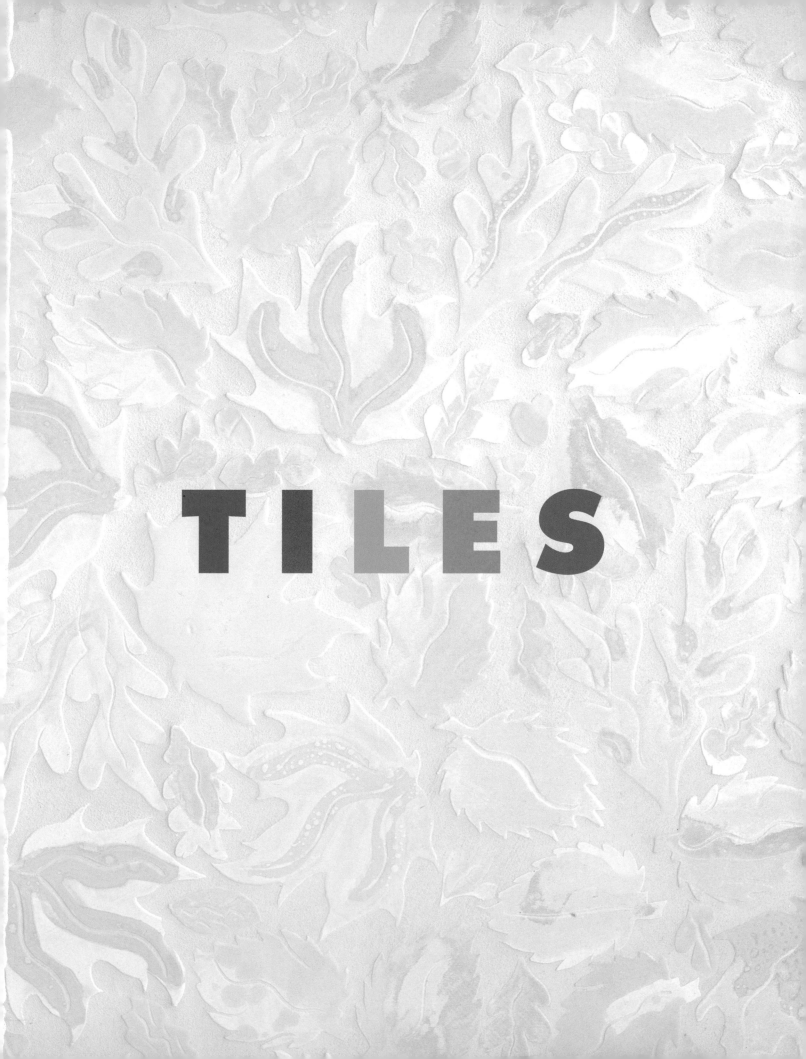

# TILES

# TILES

## CHOOSING, DESIGNING, AND LIVING WITH CERAMIC TILE

TEXT BY OLIVIA BELL BUEHL
PHOTOGRAPHS BY LISL DENNIS

*Clarkson Potter/Publishers*
*New York*

FOR OUR HUSBANDS AND FRIENDS,
RON BUEHL AND LANDT DENNIS, WHO UNDERSTOOD THAT
THIS PROJECT WAS NEVER "JUST A BOOK"

All of the photographs in this book are by Lisl Dennis except for the following. Ann Sacks Tile & Stone: 4, 18 bottom right, 82 right, 117. Lisa Bogdan: 16 and 18 top left. Country Floors: 18 bottom left and center, 63. Dal-Tile: 41. Tria Giovan: 60. Bobby Hansson: 18 top center. Liza Katz: 18 second row right. Chris Leone: 46. The Life Enhancing Tile Company: 18 third row right. The Meredith Collection: 40. Motawi Tileworks: 19, 33. Paris Ceramics: 62. Laird Plumleigh, Alchemie: 18 second row left. Walker Zanger: all trim borders on chapter openers, 18 top right and third row left and center, 53 top and bottom, and all images in the Design Workbook. Andy Warren: 26 left, 38, and 67 top. Dale Wiley, À Mano: 6.

Published by Clarkson N. Potter, Inc., 201 East 50th Street, New York, New York 10022. Member of the Crown Publishing Group.

Random House, Inc. New York, Toronto, London, Sydney, Auckland

CLARKSON POTTER, POTTER, and colophon are trademarks of Clarkson N. Potter, Inc.

http://www.randomhouse.com/

Printed in China

DESIGN BY RENATO STANISIC

Library of Congress Cataloging-in-Publication Data is available upon request.

ISBN 0-517-79976-6

10 9 8 7 6 5 4 3 2 1

First Edition

**PREVIOUS PAGES, LEFT:** Marrakesh designer Bill Willis ornamented a fireplace made of *tadelakt,* or burnished plaster, with traditional Moroccan hand-cut glazed tiles known as *zillij.* **RIGHT:** Ceramic artist Shel Neymark used the stucco exterior of his New Mexico home as a canvas for a collage of broken tile and china.

CONTENTS

# Introduction

Perhaps more than any other building material, ceramic tile captures our imaginations and produces an almost visceral response. Tile can be a sensuous medium. Our eyes are attracted to the rich colors; our fingers delight in stroking the glossy surface; our bare feet are warmed by a sun-dappled patio floor. The beauty of fired clay and its seemingly limitless variety has inspired builders for thousands of years, whether artisans who adorned the Egyptian pyramids or designers creating a mural for a skyscraper's lobby. But ancient architects would envy their present-day counterparts. Never have there been more tempting choices, with myriad craftspeople expressing their individual aesthetics in clay.

Ceramic tile is attractive not only in large expanses, but also in small accents—framing a doorway, outlining a fireplace, or lining a niche. Although tile is initially more costly than paint or wallpaper, its powerful impact —even in limited doses—makes it possible to produce stunning effects on even a beer budget. Part of tile's fascination is its paradoxical nature; for all its aesthetic appeal, tile is wonderfully durable and easy to maintain. Neither mere covering nor an integral building component, tile straddles the spheres of decoration and architecture. Tile cannot stand on its own—and a single tile is actually rather brittle—but applied to walls and floors it becomes a permanent part of the structure.

Tile is chameleonlike in its ability to express infinite variety. Fired clay yields both rough stoneware and silky smooth glazed porcelain. Modernist architect Richard Meier manipulates the rigid geometry of tile to accent his white, dramatically understated houses; Laurinda Spear and Bernardo Fort-Brescia of Miami's Arquitectonica adorn their buildings inside and out with a rainbow of ceramics. The rustic terra-cotta floors of sun-baked Tuscany suggest warmth and coziness; paradoxically, in tropical interiors, tile provides cool relief underfoot. Gleaming tiles in a restaurant kitchen bespeak modern efficiency and cleanliness, while molded tiles in earthy colors recall an era before technology defined our society. Tile can be used in intimate or grand settings; it can be simple, ornate, or fabulously funky; it can dominate a design scheme or provide a quiet backdrop.

As an architectural tool, tile can ease transitions and stylistically link one area with another—a corridor between a master bath and bedroom, for example. It can also help solve problems of scale and proportion. For instance, eight-inch tile applied as a hefty baseboard anchors a room in a way that no skinny wooden molding can. And ceramic tile is a superb mix-master, working in harmony with other natural materials such as glass, copper, wood, granite, marble, and slate, or with fabricated materials like steel, glass block, and solid surfacing.

The history of tile is entwined with the history of civilization. Ancient man discovered that wet clay would dry hard in the sun; then, undoubtedly by accident, he found that when clay was left in smoldering ashes it became harder, more water resis-

> **Each culture expresses its spirituality in clay.**
> —Ann Sacks, Ann Sacks Tile & Stone

**PRECEDING PAGE:** Old Portuguese tiles display their characteristic flamboyance on the walls of a pool house outside Lisbon. **ABOVE:** In an historic house in Makkum, the Netherlands, walls are tiled floor to ceiling with eighteenth-century murals. **OPPOSITE:** Original Malibu tiles contrast boldly with dark wood moldings in this vaulted ceiling.

tant, and able to tolerate higher temperatures than sun-baked clay. Fired clay tile was in use as a building material before recorded history. The ancient Egyptians used colored glazes more than six thousand years ago and from then on each culture has gloried in the possibilities inherent in the medium. Despite a crack here, crumbled grout there, many of the monuments to the tile artist's craft are still intact hundreds, even thousands, of years later. Over the centuries tile has covered virtually every type of surface, from the roofs of Chinese temples to the floors of Renaissance cathedrals and the facades of Colonial Mexican buildings. Tile is a democratic material. It is as likely to appear on a peasant's rough clay floor as it is in an aristocrat's ballroom. Tile has always been such an integral part of Spanish architecture that a Spanish expression for poverty, *"Es tan pobre que no tiene azulejos en su casa,"* translates as "to have a house without tile." Scandinavians treasured their tile stoves, Victorian Brits were partial to ornate tile fireplaces. More recently, the elaborately tiled walls of New York City's subway system added excitement to a new form of mass transportation.

The basic formula for making tile has changed little over

the centuries, despite technological advances that have speeded up the process, and such refinements as the ability to cut tile into almost any shape and produce tiles made of ground-up, recycled glass blended with clay. And in the electronic age, virtual reality has come to the tile showroom in the form of computer design tools that simulate how certain tiles or combinations of tiles would look in an interior.

In addition to tile's durability, it has the ability to resist heat and corrosion. When designing the space shuttle, NASA scientists selected ceramic tiles for the outer skin, which must withstand the incredible heat generated upon reentry into the atmosphere. As well as being fire resistant, tile will not emit toxic gases or fumes in a fire. Unlike carpet, wood, fabric, or paint, the color of tile is unaffected by exposure to light; unlike wallpaper, it will not peel. Tile resists dirt, since particles don't adhere to its surface—routine maintenance usually involves no more than wiping with a damp rag or sponge. Most tiles will not absorb liquids or odors, including smoke, making them hygienic; nor will they retain allergy-inducing elements. Tile can be repaired. If one tile cracks, it can be chiseled out and replaced. Many tile surfaces are nonporous and resistant to stains, making them ideal for wet places such as baths and entrance halls, and for kitchens, where grease and spills can stress many other surfaces. Tile has high thermal conductivity, meaning it is a good passive-solar collector and an excellent insulator.

Its practical virtues notwithstanding, tile's beauty and elemental appeal are responsible for its popularity. Tile suggests permanence and quality, and in our current environmental consciousness, its natural qualities are equally attractive. As the years go by, a tile's glaze may craze or a corner chip, but as the visitor to Portugal or Holland knows, such marks of age only enhance tile's natural beauty. A decade on the floor of your family room is but a moment in the life of a tile.

Although a material as enduring as tile can hardly be considered trendy, today there is a revival of interest in its use. Just as the Industrial Revolution inspired a backlash in the form of the English Arts and Crafts movement—which glorified in the unique beauty of handmade objects—the postwar obsession with technology is today giving way to a renewed interest in crafts. During the 1920s and 1930s, America was one of the largest tile producers in the world, and tile companies such as American Encaustic and Mosaic Tiling Company flourished. But the Depression drove many small companies such as Batchelder, Grueby, and Rookwood out of business. The 1940s through the 1970s represent the nadir in tile design. With most artisan companies closed, there was little to chose from but factory-made 4-inch squares in white or pastels, quarry tiles, and ceramic mosaics. So functional was the use of tile during that era that most kitchens and baths could have passed for doctors' offices. Fortunately, after a brief flirtation with plastics and other synthetic materials, we have once again come to savor the beauty, versatility, and amazing variety of fired clay.

Along with Stickley furniture that once moldered in the attic or was consigned to the Salvation Army, early-twentieth-century art pottery is now highly collectible. As we celebrate the artistic heritage of the craftsman era, contemporary artisanship is also in full flower. Encouraged by the widespread interest in handmade products, a new generation is creating glassware, pottery, and textiles, and several of the Arts and Crafts tileworks, such as Fulper and Pewabic, have reopened. Not since the 1920s, when the American Arts and Crafts era was in full flower, have so many tile artists emerged, producing wonderfully varied creations. At the turn of the century, we are witnessing nothing less than a renaissance in tile design.

As we confront the fragility of the planet, we appreciate anew the beauty and individuality of natural materials. The grain of curly maple, the texture and subtle color variation of slate, the slubs and irregularities of linen offer an appeal absent in the slick uniformity of laminate counters, vinyl floors, and permanent-press fabrics. Their very lack of perfection accounts in large part for the attraction we feel to natural materials. Made

of earth and water, nothing could be more natural than clay.

As if to celebrate this blending of art and nature, many contemporary tile artists use animal and plant motifs, much as their Arts and Crafts forebears did. Fish leap from streams, bears climb trees, and birds display their plumage, while acorns, pinecones, and leaves live forever in painted or cast images. Major manufacturers are equally influenced by this interest in natural themes. While mass-produced tiles were once plain at best, today's offerings are in a different league. Tiles that mimic the patina of age and suggest the ruins of Pompeii vie for attention with those adorned with astrological symbols. A dazzling diversity of colors, crackle glazes, and metallics provide rich choices. The interest in Spanish revival architecture has provoked reproductions of colorful Malibu and Catalina tiles. As anyone who has visited a tile supplier knows, the choice is enormous —and daunting—with offerings suitable for homes of every style. Such mind-boggling diversity is the reason for this book. In addition to American wares from artisans and major manufacturers, tile is imported from Italy, Spain, Mexico, and France. Thailand, Malaysia, Korea, Indonesia, and Brazil are also major exporters. Even Peru and Bali

make certain types of tile. Our goal is not only to acquaint you with the embarrassment of riches in the marketplace, but to offer guidance on how to successfully select and imaginatively use the ones that speak to you. Nothing could be worse than to finally pick a tile and then find—*after* it is installed in your entry hall—that it is dangerously slippery when wet, or to entrust your favorite hand-painted tile to an installer who trims it so that the design is compromised.

To gather information, we visited the studios of many of America's finest tile artists and toured high-tech American and Italian tile factories. We've been welcomed into homes with interesting installations and talked to manufacturers, artisans, tile layers, interior designers, and architects about how tile is made and used. And we've interviewed tile sales personnel to understand the ins and outs of the purchasing process.

Not encompassed in this book is the rich history of ceramic tile, on which numerous volumes have been written. Nor is this a manual on installation, for many fine books and videos already provide such information. We have excluded granite and marble tiles, which are also beautiful and popular, in order to show as rich an array of ceramic examples as possible. A few images of cement and glass tiles used like ceramics are included, as are photographs of other materials mixed with ceramics. Finally, although tile is admirably suited for commercial uses, this book will focus on residential installations.

We must admit that we have another motive in writing this book: to stamp out boring tile installations. With a material that has the potential to be so beautiful, and comes in such wondrous variety, it continues to amaze us that most people are so timid when it comes to tile. Baths and kitchens are all too often bland and unimaginative. Don't let unreasonable concerns about the resale value of your home make you opt for boredom over beauty. If your tile selection is appropriate to the rest of the design of the house, showing a little personality will not scotch a sale. The proper tile, properly installed, will provide lasting pleasure for the new owner, too. We also want to stimulate you to use tile in ways you would never have thought of. Although Americans now use considerably more ceramic tile as they did a decade ago, we still lag behind most other countries in exploiting the possibilities in the material. *Tiles* will provide you with the tools and confidence to employ this marvelous material in new ways. Be daring—go beyond kitchens and baths and use tile throughout your home, inside and out. And have some fun along the way!

**OPPOSITE:** Set in an ancient masonry wall, a new polychrome mural based on a traditional Dutch design looks as though it has graced this French courtyard for generations. **ABOVE:** Victorian English transferware tiles are highly collectible; reproductions are also available. **OVERLEAF:** Complex mosaics made from hand-cut tiles, known as *zillij*, were designed by French architect Michel Pinseau as prototypes for the Hassan II Mosque in Marrakesh.

# 1

# Fundamental Matters

*Nothing could be more basic than ceramic tile. Made of two of nature's most common materials, water and earth, it is dried in air, then transmuted by fire. The term* ceramic *refers to any mixture of clay and other nonorganic materials that is shaped and fired into a solid object.*

*A ceramic tile is designed to provide a finished surface in an architectural setting. In fact, the word* tile *comes from the Latin verb* tegere, *meaning to cover. While a tile is shaped differently from other ceramics, such as a dinner plate, coffee mug, or lamp base, its ingredients are virtually the same. Basic though tiles are, they come in an astounding variety of glazes, sizes, and shapes. A fundamental understanding of the function and performance of the different types is the key to a successful installation.*

## MANUFACTURING METHODS

Most tiles are made by one of three basic methods: They can be extruded, dust-pressed, or cast. The "green" tiles are then dried and kiln-fired, resulting in a bisque, or hard clay body. Typically, the higher the temperature, the harder and stronger, less porous, and better able to withstand extremes of temperature the tile will be. For unglazed tiles, the process is complete at this stage. Other tiles, however, are glazed and then fired again. This traditional process, which the Italians call "bicottura," fuses the glaze with the tile. Some tiles are put through yet another firing to produce a particularly unusual glaze, color combination, or design. Today, most glazed tiles are bisqued and glazed in a single trip through the kiln, a process that the Italians call "monocottura."

Handmade tiles can be rolled and cut from a sheet of damp clay or hand-formed in a frame. They can also be molded in a bas-relief or incised pattern. Compared to their machine-made cousins, handmade tiles tend to be more irregular in size, color, and thickness. Tile is usually fired in a kiln fueled by natural gas, but propane, wood, or electricity can also be used. Each type of fuel provides a different look, and various woods further vary the appearance of the glaze. Some Spanish and Italian tiles are even fired using olive pits as fuel!

Today most tiles are produced on factory assembly lines. The extrusion method forces wet clay through a die in a continuous ribbon, rather like a giant pasta maker. The ribbon is then cut into shapes, dried, and fired. Most unglazed products are made this way, although some extruded tiles are also glazed. Another factory method is dust-pressing, in which clay powders are ground, mixed, moistened, dried, and then pressed into shape with hydraulic presses that exert tons of force. Acknowledging the appeal of handmade tiles, many manufacturers now mimic their look with deliberately rounded corners, undulating surfaces, and variegated glazes.

While handmade tiles have their own charm, it comes at a price—about three times the cost of basic factory tiles and often much more. The irregularities of handmade tile can also increase installation time and labor costs. With their own distinctive aesthetic, handmade tiles are not for everyone. The slight differences from tile to tile, the fact that they are not perfectly flat and often not uniformly thick, and the idiosyncrasies of a hand-applied glaze give a rougher, more rustic look, revealing the hand of the maker. When installed, the tile's irregularity is heightened by the way light plays with the varied planes. If you are more comfortable with straight lines, exact coloration, and a perfectly flat surface, you should probably confine your selection to factory-made tiles.

Technology and more open trade agreements mean that tile from all over the world is increasingly available in every country. Italy has long been the leading tile producer as well as an innovator in style and technology. As of 1990, Italy produced about 35 percent of the world's ceramic tile, and it constitutes the largest share of imported tile sold in the United States, most of it factory-made, followed by Spain and Mexico. Handmade tile from all three countries, as well as from France, Portugal, and Great Britain, makes up a significant portion of the stock at many specialty tile outlets. Japan, Germany, and such less well known producers as Australia, New Zealand, and Wales also export fine products.

> **What is wonderful about fired clay is that it is an inherently honest material. It is exactly what it purports to be.**
>
> —Peter Soucy, Fired Clay Sales Strategies

## Making the Grade

The manufacturer's grade certifies that a tile has passed a number of dimensional and durability tests and meets appearance guidelines. Manufacturer's literature should also provide rating information. Standard-grade wall tile, ceramic mosaics, quarry tile, pavers, and special-purpose tile, marked with a blue label, have passed all requirements. Second-grade tile (seconds), indicated by a yellow label, has also passed all requirements but may have some minor defects in appearance and may differ slightly in size. Decorative thin wall tile has a similar grading system but does not include breaking strength; an orange label signifies compliance.

## EARTHY APPEAL

Some clay is used just as it is dug from the ground; most is refined to remove impurities. Clay may be mixed with ground shale or feldspar and with extenders like gypsum, talc, and sand. Depending upon its source, clay ranges in color from chalky white to brick red, with a range of grays, tans, ochers, pinks, and browns in between; the color of the wet clay does not necessarily reveal the color that will emerge after firing. Many colored clays are used for such unglazed products as terra-cotta and quarry tiles.

Glazes are almost as elemental as the clay itself, being made of ground glass, or frit, and metal oxide pigments. When glaze is heated in the kiln, it liquefies and fuses to the clay body, then hardens as it cools.

## FORM FOLLOWS FUNCTION

Tile terminology has always been somewhat confusing, with different manufacturers and different countries using various names for similar products and attributes. In addition, recent technology has produced new products—with new names— that eclipse some traditional types. As a result, some familiar terms are used loosely; others are inexact or not technically accurate. Of necessity, specific names and terms are used here, but when you communicate with a tile dealer, explain how and

where you intend to use the tile, so the salesperson can recommend appropriate choices. To be doubly certain, before ordering a specific tile, check the manufacturer's recommendations for use. If a tile is used in a way not recommended by the manufacturer, the warranty is likely to be void.

**PRECEDING PAGES, LEFT:** Bold yellow tiles, accented with rope and half-round liners and a border inspired by classical sculpture, are further enlivened by randomly placed majolica tiles in a Florida installation by Terri Levan Katz. The homeowners found compatible antique majolica plaques after the tile was installed. **CENTER:** A simple border treatment plays off handmade French field tile in mustard yellow, a favorite color in Provence. **RIGHT:** A classic Mediterranean-style border would enliven solid blue or white field tile. **THIS PAGE, LEFT:** With their flat surfaces and consistency of color and shape, white pavers accented with multicolor ceramic mosaics typify factory-made tile. **ABOVE:** In contrast, handmade field and a border of animal tiles by Moravian Pottery & Tile Works display variation in glaze, plane, even shape. The wide grout lines compensate for differences in size and shape, adding to the installation's rustic character.

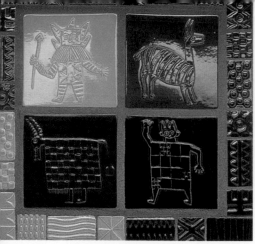

**TOP ROW, FROM LEFT:** Lynda Curtis's hand-molded and glazed stoneware tiles are inspired by West African and Australian cultures. Her shamanistic figures are painted on stoneware with stains and oxidation-fired. Part of Walker Zanger's Malibu line, the tile's glaze colors are separated by the oil-resist method. **SECOND ROW, FROM LEFT:** Laird Plumleigh's cowboy relief tile is hand-painted. A hand-painted mural was adapted from frescoes in an Etruscan tomb. **THIRD ROW, FROM LEFT:** Walker Zanger's wave design is based on an ancient graphic motif. Stonecreek's Peacock relief panel replicates a Batchelder design. Unglazed encaustic tiles are formed by inlaying damp clay in several colors before firing. **BOTTOM ROW, FROM LEFT:** Country Floors' fruit-basket is hand-painted on bisqued tile in Portugal. À Mano's maple leaf tile is carved in low relief, then glazed. Busby Gilbert's Art Nouveau Poppy uses raised relief to keep glazes from merging. **OPPOSITE:** Molded dragonfly tile is from Motawi's Art Nouveau line.

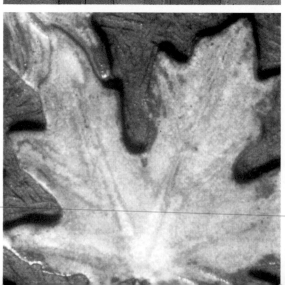

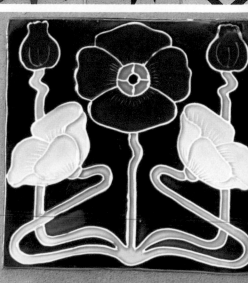

These caveats notwithstanding, it is useful to have a working knowledge of some of the terminology commonly used to describe tiles and their properties. Basically, the industry has established product categories based upon the way tile is manufactured, its breaking strength, and size. The four main types are quarry tile, pavers, mosaics, and glazed wall tile. Quarry tile is made by the extrusion process, pavers by the dust-pressed method; both are 6 square inches or more, may be glazed or unglazed, and have a breaking strength that makes them suitable for use on floors. Ceramic mosaics can be made by either

method, are glazed or unglazed, and are always smaller than 6 square inches. Some mosaics are strong enough to use on both floors and walls, others are suitable only for walls. Glazed wall tile, again at least 6 square inches, has a breaking strength less than is necessary for floor tile and is suitable for interior use only.

There is also a category the industry calls special-purpose tile, which covers tiles made for specific uses. Certain imported or handcrafted tiles, including encaustics and terra-cotta, which do not fall neatly into any of the four main groups, are also included in this category without indicating that they are inferior in quality. Finally, a category called decorative wall tile includes products with a lesser breaking strength than regular wall tile.

Many tiles, such as porcelain, ceramic mosaics, and vitrified products, can be used on both floors and walls. Other tiles are location specific. Almost any tile can be used on walls, but floors and counters need tiles with added strength. Again, the manufacturer's recommendations for usage should be your guide.

Floor tiles, whether glazed or unglazed, are made to endure scratching and weight that wall tiles don't have to handle. In technical terms, the breaking strength of floor tile is considerably greater than that of wall tile. (Greater thickness does not denote higher breaking strength; floor tiles range from

¼ inch to 1 inch thick.) Specialized tiles, such as those with slip-resistant surfaces, are also available. For exterior wet areas or areas adjoining the outdoors, many slip-resistant tiles have Carborundum or abrasive grit added to the surface; others employ wire-cut surfaces, grooves, textures, or raised treads.

Generally about ¼ to 5/16 inch thick, glazed wall tile need not be as strong as floor tile, since it will not be walked on. Its softer body makes it relatively easy to cut to accommodate plumbing outlets and the like. Its glaze is not expected to withstand too much abrasion. Decorative glazed wall tile is suitable for walls and backsplashes but never has the breaking strength necessary for counter use. Various names used in different countries for wall tiles include majolica, faience, delftware, earthenware, cotto, and whiteware. (Some glazed wall tiles are suitable for indoor floors that receive only light use, or as accents with other tiles.)

The weight of a tile depends upon the clay body and its thickness, ranging from 2 to 3 pounds per square foot for wall tile up to 4 to 5 pounds per square foot for floor tile. Some terra cotta can weigh more than 8 pounds per square foot.

## THE RATINGS GAME

To help determine proper usage, many tiles are rated and graded (see Making the Grade, page 16). The ratings reflect physical properties, while the grade ascertains quality compliance. Different countries have traditionally used different systems to rate tiles, often making it difficult to compare domestic and imported products, although plans are underway to have most countries conform to a single rating system determined by the International Standards Organization (ISO).

Standards established by the American National Standards Institute (ANSI) define the physical properties of tile. One important standard rates porosity, or permeability, and is to a large extent

• *Vitreous:* Water absorption rate of more than 0.5 percent but less than 3 percent.

• *Semivitreous:* Water absorption rate of more than 3 percent but less than 7 percent.

• *Nonvitreous:* Water absorption rate of more than 7 percent.

Tiles rated impervious are suitable for use in wet and frost-prone areas, are usually stain resistant, and can generally withstand heavy use. Vitreous tiles are suitable for interior and most exterior floors subject to water and can usually handle heavy loads without cracking. Semivitreous tiles are generally not recommended for outside use because absorbed water could freeze and crack tile. Nonvitreous tiles are highly absorbent, usually making them a poor choice for wet areas or exterior installations.

In general, glazed tiles will resist water and household stains from food and cleaning products, although some special glazes or designs may be affected by acids and other caustic agents. Unglazed impervious tiles are also stain-resistant, but other unglazed products, including porcelain, may need to be sealed. Check the manufacturer's recommendations.

Almost any tile can be used on walls and backsplashes, but those used on floors, kitchen counters, and other work areas need to be strong enough to resist scratches. Both the International Standards Organization and American National Standards Institute's standards rate resistance to surface abrasion or glaze hardness (for glazed floor tiles) and resistance to deep abrasion

the key to understanding appropriate usage. Porosity depends largely upon the way the tile is fired. Low-fired clay can be filled with more air pockets that absorb water and therefore tends to have a higher absorption rate. A longer and hotter firing usually results in a lower porosity. High-fired tiles usually have a denser, stronger body that is also more impermeable to stains, a key consideration in kitchens; some can be used in outdoor situations where freezing cycles occur.

The four ANSI categories of porosity range from those that for all practical purposes do not absorb water to those increasingly apt to absorb moisture, as follows:

• *Impervious:* Water absorption rate of 0.5 percent or less.

**FAR LEFT:** Opaque glazes in autumnal hues are among more than 500 options from Pewabic Pottery. Bullnose-edge tiles navigate the transition from the hearth to the vertical plane below. **LEFT:** In a contemporary kitchen, lustrous glazed tiles by Fire & Earth glimmer with coppery highlights. **OPPOSITE:** The naturalism of Natalie Surving's subjects are heightened by satin glazes, part of a 20-step decorative process. **OVERLEAF:** In a Southwestern kitchen, cobalt blue Mexican Talavera tiles define the chimney breast. On flanking walls is a repeat pattern of blue-and-white squares; solid blue reappears behind the hanging cupboards.

(for unglazed floor tiles). Abrasion resistance does not apply to wall tile.

Glazed tiles are rated by the Porcelain Enamel Institute (PEI) system, ranging from I to V, to determine appropriate usage. Higher numbers indicate higher resistance and a more scratch-resistant glaze. Class I is suitable for walls only. A tile with a rating of II could suffice as flooring in a bath off a bedroom, and III or IV is essential in baths opening off main living areas, and for entryways, family rooms, and kitchens. Class V is necessary only in commercial settings, but can also be used in a home.

Important as ratings are, a multitude of factors determine appropriate usage. Certain semivitreous tiles, for example, can be used outdoors satisfactorily. Consumers should rely on manufacturers' recommendations for specific uses.

## ALL THE TRIMMINGS

Tile retailers stock a variety of practical and decorative trim tiles. The former include the special pieces used at the borders of an installation to ease the transition to plaster or other materials and to negotiate edges and corners. Bullnose trim, for example, curves to accommodate an outside right angle. The glazed edges of such pieces also provide greater resistance to water absorption and breakage than field tile. Special curved-nose stair-step tread tiles are designed to lay horizontally and overlap a step kick, or riser. The stair step may feature a strip of slip-resistant ribbing for added safety.

Decorative trims are the borders and narrow strips, or liners, called *listellos* in Italian, that can turn an otherwise ordinary installation into an extraordinary one. In fact, in a contemporary house lacking in architectural detail, tile can fill the void. It's not necessary to restrict your options to coordinated tiles; you can use a border from one manufacturer and a field tile from another, or pair a handmade border with a factory-made field tile. In fact, a calculated mix of colors and textures can produce splendid results. (If you choose a trim that coordinates with your field tile, be sure to purchase it at the same time to ensure matched tones and textures.) Feel free to mix tiles, but watch out for differences in thickness and size. Tiles from different manufacturers can have the same nominal size but may differ slightly in actual size. Minor differences in thickness are usu-

## Neat and Trim

Properly selected trim tile gives any installation a clean line and facilitates cleaning. The most common types of functional (as opposed to decorative) trim tile are:

• **Bullnose**—Rounded top edge used as the last tile in a wall installation that doesn't extend to the ceiling or up to the cabinet line, or to turn an outside edge. A bullnose for a mud-set installation has a deeper curve than that for thin-set. A double bullnose has two rounded edges to navigate a corner.

• **Cove**—Curved concavely to join flush with floor tile or form an inside corner.

• **Bead**—A narrow, convexly curved piece designed to turn an outside corner.

• **Inside corner**—A thin piece that curves concavely to handle an inside corner.

• **Base trim**—Curved concavely on the bottom to meet flush with floor tile and with a bullnose at the top for a clean finish. Also called a round-top cove base.

• **V-cap**—Curved edge used on the front edge of a counter to prevent spillage. Also known as counter trim or no-drip counter edge.

• **Quarter round**—Used to create continuity where 90-degree angles occur.

• **Half round**—Thin semicylindrical pieces used as decorative accents or to frame or separate areas.

• **Windowsill**—Also known as step nosing, used to provide a rounded surface where two planes meet at a windowsill or stair tread.

**ABOVE:** Ridged terra-cotta step nosing trim, known as coping when used beside a pool, negotiates the transition from the patio tiles to the vertical plane. The textured tile, also used on the pool steps, minimizes the risk of slipping on wet surfaces. Malibu Potteries tiles appear as a border and at the waterline. **OPPOSITE:** A latticework design in four colors of Peace Valley mosaic tile is separated from companion field tile by a border depicting Celtic knots.

ally all right when the edges are glazed. But without glazed edges, varying thicknesses could stress the glaze on the thicker tile; significant differences will require compensation during installation.

An alternative to trim pieces, which can be costly—or unavailable in your chosen color or design—is to cut field tile pieces to fit. This practice has been customary in Europe, although foreign manufacturers are now making more trim pieces than they used to. Mitered tiles (meaning that edges are cut at 45-degree angles so two pieces can be butted together to create a flush, finished edge) are used for outside corners. Some tiles can be ordered with mitered edges, or they can be cut on site. A highly skilled installer can often cut tile to solve many of the situations that specialty trims handle. But mitered corners will not wear as well as bullnose trim in high-use areas. Another option is to special-order tiles with glazed edges, a good solution when you want the tile to meet a wall surface or turn an outside corner and trim pieces aren't available.

## COMPONENTS OF DESIGN

When choosing tile it is virtually impossible to react only to color, texture, decoration, size, or shape, because these design components are as inextricably linked as glaze to fired clay. But it is worth looking at each component individually in order to fully grasp the diverse effects that can be achieved with tile.

### Color

Solid-color tiles derive their hues from the clay itself, the glaze, and the firing process. Different clays provide significant variety in the coloration, surface appearance, and finishes of

quarry tile and terra cotta. Unglazed porcelain tile comes in a wide range of pastels and bold colors achieved by dispersing mineral oxides throughout the clay before firing.

Glazed tile offers far greater color options. (Some companies even will custom-color tile to match a fabric or wallpaper, assuming a minimum order.) Glaze is made of glass, tinted with mineral oxides, and fluxes, or fuses, to the clay. The glass reflects light, giving an intensity of color that is positively jewel-like. Colored glazes can be opaque, translucent, or almost transparent with matte, low-gloss, satin, high-gloss, or textured finishes.

Some glazes are uniform; others display mottling, a network of fine crackle lines, or another deliberately imperfect look. Such variation can occur both within the borders of one tile and from tile to tile, even among those fired at the same time. Other techniques lend the appearance of texture to tile surfaces. For example, pools of color in a shiny glaze can give the impres-

sion of depth; a sponged-on glaze also belies its smooth surface. Some matte glazes involve up to five or six layers of irregularly applied colors to mimic the look of granite or slate. A sprayed-on finish produces natural variation; silk-screened versions employ one or more overprints to give the illusion of variation. Other faux finishes imitate leather or wood.

## *Texture and Relief*

Actual texture on the tile surface adds another dimension to color. Texture also serves the practical purpose of providing the slip-resistant surface essential for entries, bathroom floors, and areas around pools. Texture is achieved both in the clay itself and through the use of glazes. The rough surface of an unglazed paver can result from the use of clay with a lot of grit. Dusting a glaze with finely ground sand adds a rustic texture.

Other ways to create surface interest include stamping, imprinting a textured material such as burlap, or carving damp or

**ABOVE:** Pewter-finish tile from Ann Sacks in a wafflelike grid overlaid with diagonal lines adds textural interest to a contemporary kitchen. **LEFT:** In a tiled niche, 4-inch pumpkin-color squares are framed with a checkerboard of maroon and blue ceramic mosaics, which itself is banded in maroon trim. The high-contrast color combination is typical of North African design. **OPPOSITE:** Frank Giorgini's hand-molded tiles based on African textile designs and lizards are oxidation-fired with a black glaze on a tan stoneware body.

partially dried clay. Incised areas allow the glaze to puddle, adding to the texture. Some tiles imprint actual leaves, flowers, and herbs into the clay. Raised relief designs are formed by using a mold to press damp clay into a three-dimensional shape. Some relief tiles are hand-painted to enhance their verisimilitude. A cleverly textured or relief tile can look handmade, even if it is crafted under factory conditions. Textured tiles often coordinate better with a material such as granite than decorated ones, which tend to dominate a design scheme. Finally, texture works well in contemporary settings, where traditional designs often seem overly fussy.

## Decoration

Hand-painted tiles from around the world in a wide range of designs make up much of the stock at specialty tile shops. Hand-painted tile has a very strong personality, so be sure that the artist's sensibility is close to your own. Highly decorated tile also can "fight" with other design components if not carefully planned in advance.

As distinguished from decorative glazing, designs may be hand-painted, silk-screened, stenciled, or applied with decals. Decoration can be applied directly to a bisque tile, a process

## Gruen kern Soup

Soak whole grünkern overnight
Dry well
Roast in frying pan
with a little oil
rock pot with lean
and onion

Friday

May be used for
Friday night m
Shabbat lunch.

· BEANS · SU GAR

called underglaze painting; a second firing fixes the glaze and protects the painted decoration. In overglaze painting, an artist applies decoration over a transparent or solid-color glaze before a final firing.

Some decorated tiles rely on relief to separate the colored glazes. The artisan fills a tube with liquid clay, known as slip, to draw a design in thin raised lines. After the slip dries, the applied glazes puddle between the tube lines. Alternatively, an oil pen that "resists" the glazes is used between colors to keep them distinct.

Stenciled designs can be applied by using an acetate or metal mask and brushing or spraying glaze over the cut-out area. Slight variations from tile to tile add to the hand-crafted look.

Most factory-made decorated tile is silk-screened. Once a bisque tile is glazed and dry, the design is applied with one or more mesh screens (one for each color) in a fashion similar to silk-screening onto paper. A transparent overglaze may follow before the tile is kiln-fired. Silk-screened tiles tend to have a uniform look.

Finally, decals made of thin paper or acetate can be used to transfer a design to a bisqued or glazed tile, which is then refired to bond the design to the tile.

To many people, the term *decorated tile* immediately conjures up images of fanciful depictions of flowers, fruits, farm animals, and other naive subjects that adorn many a country-style kitchen. Traditional Portuguese *culinarios,* for example, display a more diverse selection of fruits and vegetables than you'd find in a well-stocked supermarket. But you'll also find such subjects as hot-air balloons, scenes from classical Greek mythology, and Navajo motifs. Geometric and abstract designs are particularly suited to contemporary interiors.

### Size

Tile size plays a dominant role in the appearance of a room. Particularly effective is the use of several sizes, such as 2-, 4-, and 8-inch squares arranged in a design that allows joint alignment. At one time, 4¼-inch-by-4¼-inch wall tile was the

## The Custom Route

If you are unable to find a tile that "speaks to you," consider commissioning hand-painted tiles. An artist can provide a unique design based upon your interests, favorite colors, hobbies, pets, a memorable vacation, or perhaps to coordinate with a fabric. Usually, you can have the design painted on factory-made blanks, allowing you to mix hand-painted tiles or a mural with stock pieces, an aid in keeping the price within reason.

Typically, a tile artist oversees the installation to make sure that the pieces are laid properly. While such custom projects do not come cheap, they ensure a unique design that is imbued with personal meaning. Custom tile artists can be found through interior designers, architects, or kitchen and bath dealers. Some tile showrooms and even major manufacturers will take on custom work if the project is large enough. As with any custom work, the best way to find someone whose work you like and who will deliver on time is through personal recommendations.

**OPPOSITE:** Custom tiles were bisqued, painted, and refired by Marion Grebow, who depicted the homeowner's favorite foods on a backsplash. Calligraphy decals of recipes and ingredients were transferred onto companion tiles in the firing process. **ABOVE:** For a horse-owning family, artist Phyllis Traynor painted a charming—and fortunately fruitless—fox hunt, part of a mural that extends around the backsplash and onto the range hood, on bisqued stock tile, then refired it.

norm, but in recent years 6-inch-by-6-inch tiles have enjoyed increased popularity. Likewise, the standard 6-inch square floor tile is giving way to larger squares. Mosaic tiles are also being used in innovative ways. Tile is actually sold in nominal sizes, much as lumber is, meaning, for example, that a so-called 6-by-6-inch tile can actually be 5¾ inches by 5¾ inches. (The size can vary slightly from one manufacturer to another and from run to run. If you are mixing tiles from different manufacturers, be sure the actual sizes are the same.) The tile box or specification sheet will give the nominal dimensions, including thickness. European tile is produced in metric dimensions, but measurements are converted into the equivalent number of inches; again, check the *actual* size.

Practical considerations also come into play when choosing a size. A surface must be relatively flat and true to allow a larger tile to adhere and not crack, plus its added weight must be considered (a larger floor tile may require a mud-set or a leveling agent). In a very small room or narrow corridor, an extra-large tile may be wasted, since there will be space for only a few full rows.

## *S h a p e*

Tiles come in squares, rectangles, diamonds, hexagons, octagons, even rhomboids and triangles. Some companies now offer triangles in various sizes, and some offer square tiles that are scored, allowing the installer to strike them firmly to get a clean triangular cut, eliminating the need to laboriously cut squares in half in order to create triangles for turning corners

and creating geometric borders. Handmade tiles may even be formed into the shape of a leaf, a fish, or another object designed to fit into a field of tile or to marry with companion pieces.

Size, shape, glaze—each of these factors plays on the others to create an overall impression. The next chapter offers more food for thought on creating effective designs in tile.

**Opposite, Above:** Michelle Griffoul's spirals, crescents, triangles, circles, and other fancifully shaped tiles are cut, glazed, fired, and then mounted on net in colorful mosaics; grout becomes a key design element. **Opposite, Below:** By mixing colors and sizes of rectangles, triangles, and squares in a multilayer border, a floor in the traditional octagon and dot pattern becomes increasingly intricate. **Below:** Terra-cotta hexagons and glazed triangles depicting phoenixes combine to form six-pointed stars.

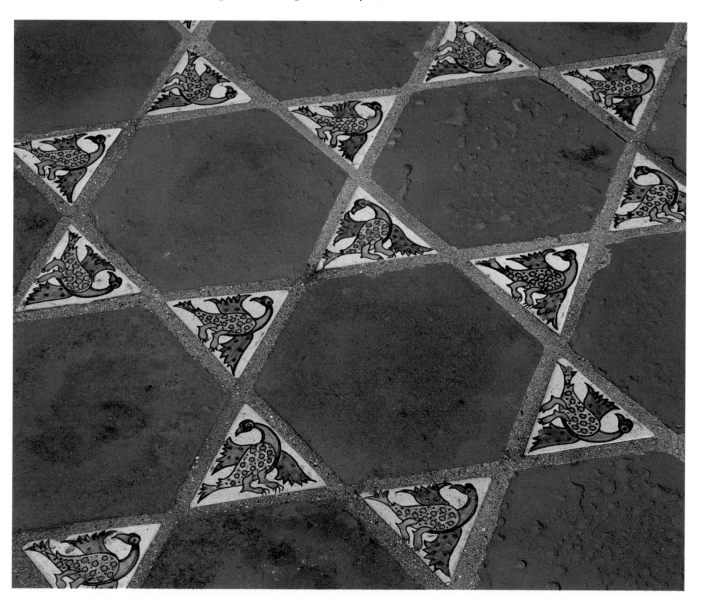

# 2

# Putting It All Together

Despite its strength as a design component, ceramic tile must never be regarded in isolation. Even in a bathroom tiled from floor to ceiling, fixtures, fittings, mirrors, and cabinetry are intimately related to the ceramic surfaces. Whether it is the dominant element of a room or a subtle backdrop, tile is always an active partner in an assemblage of other materials and patterns.

You can either link tile to existing decor or use it as the starting point to establish a look. Tiles have the ability to immediately suggest an era or a particular mood. For example, Victorian rooms often featured relief tiles that depicted ornate naturalistic or classical themes. Tiny hexagons and rectangular "subway" tiles evoke baths from the 1920s and 30s, and overscale squares exemplify the "less is more" ethic of much contemporary design.

Lozenges and curvaceous shapes immediately suggest a Mediterranean sensibility. As for mood, matte or textured handmade tiles create a more informal atmosphere than glossy, highly finished ones. The way in which tile is installed adds another rich layer of possibilities. For example, solid-color squares laid corner to corner present a simple geometric pattern; but offset them half a tile to produce a running-bond pattern, and you get a wholly different look. Use white grout with white tile to establish a classic impression; substitute red grout, and the effect becomes bold, playful, and contemporary. When tiles of more than one color, texture, shape, or design are combined, the options increase geometrically.

If you want tile to define the room, it's better to delay other design decisions until you have selected your tile. On the other hand, if tile is to be subordinated to a fabric pattern, for example, select ceramics in complementary colors or a subtle pattern that does not "fight" the fabric. The most difficult design scheme to pull off is the use of tile as an equal partner with other textures and/or materials, although it can be enormously effective when done well. For instance, one could use relief tiles decorated with circles, triangles, and squares as fireplace and door surrounds, then choose a woven fabric incorporating the same forms. An etched glass coffee-table top might reiterate one of the shapes and the border of the parquet floor another. Each component is related to the others, but none overpowers.

Feel free to use tile with granite or another stone, glass block, or wallcovering. The most interesting design schemes consciously mix materials to contrast colors and textures. Just as the slickness of glass is heightened by the roughness of a wicker chair, the suedelike finish of tumbled marble against the sheen of a glazed tile can be as pleasing to the touch as it is to the eye. Similarly, panels of earthy, handmade tile bordered by planks of pickled redwood establish a dialogue between two natural textures. An all-marble bath may be elegant but cold; but play peach-hued ceramic wall tiles against a beige marble tub deck and floor, and the room becomes warm and inviting.

Rely on repetition for impact. For instance, embrace a tile

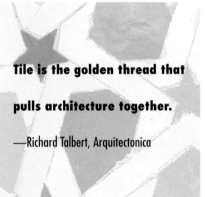

**Tile is the golden thread that pulls architecture together.**

—Richard Talbert, Arquitectonica

counter with a frame of solid surfacing, then inset tile into a shower stall of the same material. Or repeat tile used on a backsplash as a dado in a breakfast nook. Such details unite not only the materials but the various areas of the room. When mixing materials, junctures where the two meet should always be carefully planned. For instance, if you are using glass block within a shower area in a bath otherwise covered with tile, consider whether the shape of the glass block should reiterate the tile or make a different statement. And plan out if or how the joints of the glass block will align with those of the tile.

Some tiles have such a strong personality that one must simply give them their head. A multicolored tile patchwork quilt will not brook much intervention from other elements. If you use bold tile in a niche, why spoil your viewing pleasure with wood shelves? Instead, use transparent glass shelves so that the design can be fully appreciated. Tile that is strongly associated with a certain era is usually most comfortable with traditional furnishings and finishes that complement it. Reproduction Portuguese *azulejos* or delft tiles will feel at home with traditional wood cabinets, brass hardware, and antique furniture. Mexican Talavera tiles, in turn, immediately suggest a more informal, rustic setting, with companion materials like sandblasted pine, barn siding, or pierced tin.

Collect samples of all the materials you are interested in using before making any hard-and-fast decisions. Take a tip from designers, who attach the various materials and paint colors to a board so they can view them in relation to one another. That way you'll be able to look at that small-print wallcovering against a floral tile to see whether the two will engage in mortal combat or coexist peacefully. Even though you may love components individually, two or more patterns simply may not work well in the same space. In such cases, you may want to use one in an adjoining room, or to confine it to a minor note, a border, say, instead of a whole wall. In general, such classic patterns as checkerboards, stripes, and lattice weaves, especially when used in subtle, low-contrast colors, are the easiest to marry with other patterns.

PRECEDING PAGES, LEFT: Designer Fernando Sanchez of The Pineapple Design chose tiles depicting his company's namesake for his Miami kitchen. Reproductions of William De Morgan's nineteenth-century transferware tiles, themselves inspired by Turkish and Persian designs, are complemented by wine red walls, wood graining on the cabinets, and the stone window frame. CENTER: The multicolor Celtic motif medallion hand-molded by Motawi Tileworks depicts doves surrounded by dogs chasing stags. RIGHT: This curvaceous border design works equally well in horizontal and vertical applications. THIS PAGE, ABOVE: Malibu tiles inspired by traditional Mediterranean and Moorish designs lend colorful character to the kitchen in the Adamson House, once home to the owners of the Malibu Potteries and now a tile museum.

## PATTERN AND COLOR

The urge to manipulate colors and shapes into complex designs reflects our eternal quest for beauty. Pattern, meaning the arrangement of tiles, as distinguished from the decoration of an individual tile, played an enormous role in the history of tiles. Ancient Persians formed intricate nonrepresentational patterns from tiles of different colors. Pattern continues to be a powerful design element today, although it need not be complex to be compelling. Tiles lend themselves beautifully to patterns as basic as a checkerboard or a chevron. Classic Provençal kitchens are often decorated with hunter green or golden yellow tiles played off white companions. The Portuguese delight in arranging their primary-hued tiles in graphic patterns. Mexicans play visual geometric tricks by glazing square tiles with white and another color to create two triangles which can then be combined in animated and intricate designs. (For more on designing patterns, see Pattern Play, page 170.)

The usual rules about color and pattern apply to tiles much as they do to fabrics, wallpaper, and paint colors. Specifically, dark colors tend to make spaces look smaller; paler tones open them up. Rooms without much natural light or with a northern exposure can benefit from the warming qualities of sunny colors and pale tones, while south-facing rooms can handle cool or darker colors. Likewise, a busy pattern or a mix of colors

**OPPOSITE:** Inspired by Moroccan interiors, designers Jed Johnson and Scott Cornelius applied an elaborate tapestry of sizes and shapes of glazed and unglazed Peace Valley tiles to the fireplace, walls, and floors of a sitting room at Twin Farms in Barnard, Vermont. **ABOVE:** A close-up in the adjoining hall reveals how the pattern was carefully planned to maintain symmetry and minimize cuts. **OVERLEAF:** In the kitchen of a restored house in the south of France, locally made glazed green and white tiles form a traditional harlequin pattern on wainscot and backsplash.

creates a sense of confinement. On the other hand, loose, open patterns and monochromatic color schemes in pale tones create a sense of airiness. Bright colors energize social areas; pale colors provide relaxation in personal spaces.

But like all rules, design principles are meant to be broken, as indeed they are with great frequency by the most innovative designers. A bold design or color can be dramatic or cozy when deliberately used in a powder room or other small space. Similarly, a rich, dark color creates a lushness and excitement in a room that is used infrequently or only at night.

## COLOR COMBINATIONS

Region and climate also influence design decisions. People who live in hot, dry climates, for example, are often attracted to the pale colors that reflect light and heat; denizens of northern climes find that rich, more saturated colors provide the illusion of warmth.

No color lives in a vacuum. Leonardo da Vinci was perhaps the first to explain that each color is affected by the colors around it, writing in his *Treatise of Painting* that white will appear brightest next to black. And long before Sir Isaac Newton designed the color wheel, da Vinci observed that the opposite colors like green and red will heighten each other's effect. Likewise, lavender and yellow create maximum impact.

If you prefer less dramatic contrasts, consider pairing one full-strength color with a toned-down partner, cobalt blue, for example, with pale peach, or combine celadon green with terra cotta. Using the toned-down color as the field tile and the bolder one as a border will create a completely different effect than when the relationship is reversed. Or you may feel more comfortable opting for pastel or grayed versions of both colors.

There is beauty in harmony as well as in contrast. Da Vinci went on to explain that colors that are close to each other, blue and green, for example, are a pleasing combination, as are yellow and orange or violet and red. Again, consider these combinations not just in their full strengths but also the whole range of pale to dark tones. Don't stop with two. Three or more colors can work in bold or gentle combinations. Or go for the impact of one color, but vary the finish—high gloss, satin, or matte—alternating them to form a subtle yet distinct pattern.

If you are attracted to a color but are not sure you will be as fond of it years from now, consider using it in moderation as an accent with a neutral color. Classic combinations such as blue and white are always in style. One way to enliven such a basic color scheme is to add an accent of another, unexpected color. When it comes to color choices, follow your natural inclinations and consider what you already own. Your clothes and other possessions are a good clue to what colors you feel comfortable living with.

If you are building from scratch or embarking upon a major renovation, you may be eager to create a completely new color scheme. But if you are only replacing the floor in your kitchen, clearly you will want to take into consideration the hue of the cabinets and the color and pattern of the counters when selecting tile. Also keep in mind the color scheme in adjoining rooms. The White House may be able

**OPPOSITE:** Surrounding a banquette, argyle tile patterns the floor, jewel tones define a wall niche, and floral designs climb the wall, their several patterns mixing with those of the fabrics and finishes to establish an exotic ambience. **LEFT:** In contrast, in a compact kitchen, tile counters and backsplashes of slightly pillowed tile in a checkerboard pattern dominate the design. The refrigerator is painted to mimic tile.

to handle a red room, a blue room, and a gold room, but in today's often open-plan homes, abrupt shifts in color may prove disruptive. In linked spaces, reiterating a tile element can lend a harmonizing effect. For example, consider repeating the tile used on a kitchen backsplash on the fireplace surround in the adjoining family room. Likewise, you will probably want the colors in your master bath to have a relationship to those in the bedroom, even if the materials are different.

In your efforts to coordinate tiles with other materials and products, you'll find assistance from many manufacturers and tile distributors. Some large companies present coordinated collections that make it easy to pick wall and floor tiles that go together. A good selection of borders and other decorative trims allow individuality within a color-linked grouping. These same companies have also joined up with manufacturers of plumbing fixtures and makers of wallcovering, laminate, and solid surfacing, to coordinate colors of products commonly used in kitchens and baths.

In practical terms, extremely pale colors and dark colors are harder to keep looking clean than midrange tones. So are solid colors, as opposed to subtle patterns, which are natural dirt hiders. Dark glazed tiles are more apt to show scratches from heavy traffic and other damage, another important consideration if you have young children, pets, or live in an area where mud or sand is frequently tracked into the house.

**ABOVE:** Sleek white Italian tiles are fitted with stainless steel grommets. **LEFT:** Handmade field and border tile wears a translucent white glaze that takes on a pinky tinge from the terra-cotta bisque below. **BELOW:** Alternating plain white and geometric relief squares create a dynamic pattern, heightened by a coordinated border. **OPPOSITE:** Tiny white ceramic mosaics wrap around shelves, soffits, and counter edges; dark gray grout defines the tiles' unusual shape. **OVERLEAF:** Designer Gail Green tiled a master bath floor to ceiling with large white tiles, then accented them with smaller squares made from a checkerboard of sea shell chips. Floor tile, laid diagonally, is bordered in a slim black band.

## THE SIMPLE POWER OF WHITE

In spite of all the colors, decorations, and patterns possible in tile, there is one look that remains popular in stark contrast to these bold worlds of opportunity. Whether a pure chalk, yellow-tinged ivory, skim-milk blue, or peachy cream, white is still the favorite (non)color in paint, tile, and many other decorative materials. White and its kissing cousins can create a dramatic environment or a subtle, peaceful, almost meditative one.

The danger of an all-white scheme is boredom. There's a

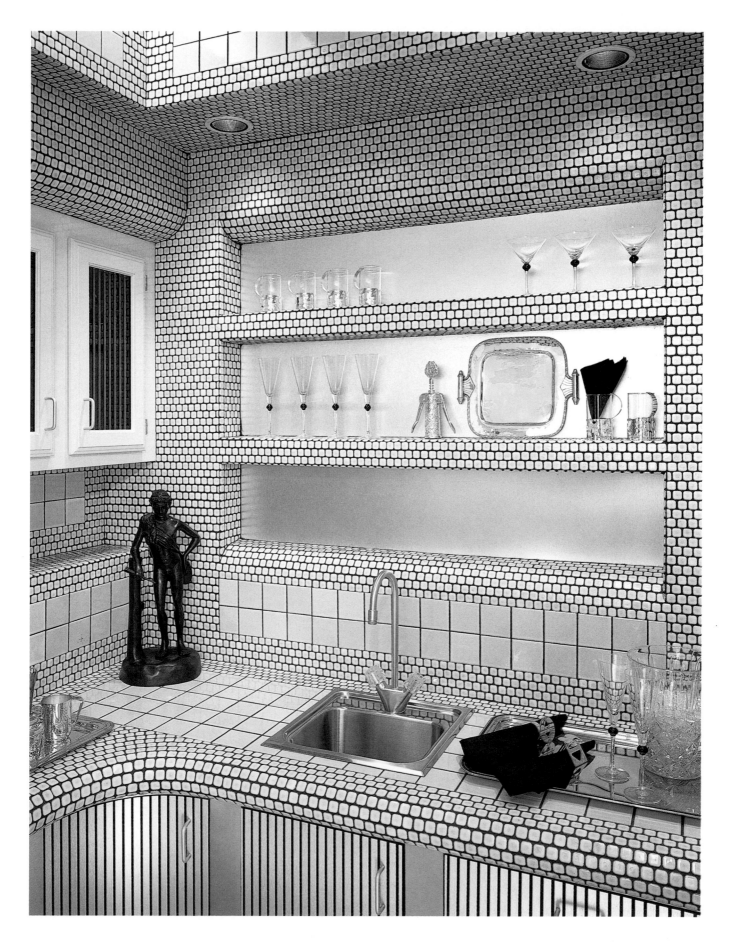

thin line between serene and dull, between dramatic and sterile. If you are attracted to white, make sure that you have enough going on in the space to add visual interest, whether in the design of the tile itself, the graceful curve of a pedestal sink, or contrast with wallcovering. The detail that creates interest can be understated, a simple white rope border used to accent white field tile laid on the diagonal, for example. There is also one clear disadvantage to white: Dirt cannot hide in a white space. If you are not in the running for world's neatest housekeeper, think twice before installing an all-white kitchen or bath. On the plus side, white can be beautiful, and it is as basic in decorating as black is in fashion. Because of its timeless quality, all-white or white in combination with another color is at home in any style home or room. From the simple charm of a cottage look to a more sophisticated setting, white has a timeless appeal.

A white scheme can also serve a more practical purpose, making any space seem larger. White lightens a dark room, reflecting and maximizing any available light. And white can also "erase" irregularities and less-than-ideal architecture. The color has the ability to make something out of nothing, more out of less. Just as a piece of furniture lacking graceful lines suddenly acquires charm when given a coat of crisp white paint, a small bath with odd angles and perhaps a radiator that can't be eliminated takes on a pristine beauty when tiled floor to ceiling in simple white tile.

Since much of all tile sold is white or off-white, manufacturers offer enormous options. Shapes range from tiny circles and classic "hexes" to triangles, octagons, crescents, and, of course, squares and rectangles of every size. Raised relief moldings abound. From the simplicity of unpolished white porcelain to the poached-egg-white look of an almost transparent glaze, the range of surface effects is equally dazzling. Tone-on-tone or other self-patterns include dots, checks, or stripes, which also can be incised or molded. Each shape, size, and glaze has its own distinct personality, hinting at appropriate uses. A white-glazed raku tile with its distinctive black cracks suggests a contemplative Oriental setting; a classical Grecian relief in a creamy white conjures up a more formal environment.

A note on mixing and matching whites: Just as wool and cotton will never take dye exactly the same way, the white of ceramic tile will not necessarily match the white of a painted cabinet, an epoxy-finished faucet, a fiberglass tub, or an enameled sink. Painted white surfaces will yellow with exposure to sunlight. Even whites on different surfaces or composed of different materials that may look the same at first glance reflect light differently when installed, some on vertical, some on horizontal surfaces. Rather than drive yourself crazy trying to match everything perfectly, take a tip from designers who recommend a mixture of whites for added interest. That way, your monochromatic space will continue to look fresh for years to come.

## WHITE AND WHATEVER

White is the most sociable of colors: It heightens and gives definition to every other color, whether in delicate contrast, such as with pale blue, or in powerful opposition, as with red. Such pairings can be boldly graphic or elegantly discreet. Black and white, the high-contrast color combination, like all classics, works equally well in traditional and contemporary designs. An equally dramatic combination is the mix of white-glazed and natural unglazed terra cotta, a contrast heightened by the textural play of satiny smooth and ever-so-slightly rough. White glazed ceramic is also a traditional foil for granite and marble.

## NEUTRAL BUT NICE

White's relatives, cream, gray, beige, and the darker earth tones, are also perennially popular, and they work well as field tiles with equally subtle or more vibrantly colored accents. Like white, neutrals are easy to live with, but they are easier to maintain. Reflecting a strong interest in the environment, earth tones are in vogue again. And for homeowners with resale concerns, neutrals have the advantage of running little risk of offending would-be purchasers. Fortunately, neutral need not be synonymous with boring. Simply mixing quarry tiles in several natural

colors can be enormously effective. Terra-cotta pavers stained in different shades can be used in similar fashion.

Expand your definition of neutral to include glazed tiles that mimic the look of marble, granite, lichen-covered stone, or even leather, which make up in textural appeal what they may lack in bold color. Or experiment with the elegant but neutral metallic tones of gold, silver, copper, pewter, and bronze, perhaps with bluish green anodized accents. A bath clad in pewter-glazed tiles takes on a masculine look, but when used as a border with pale or white field tile, metallics can assume a more delicate look.

**OPPOSITE:** To serve as an understated backdrop for the master bathroom's matchless view of the Pacific Ocean, the owners of this southern California house opted for classic white rectangular tiles, laid in an equally classic running bond pattern. **ABOVE:** Jewel-tone glass tiles enliven white ceramic tiles in this shower with built-in stool.

# SCALE AND PROPORTION

When it comes to scale (the actual size of an object) and proportion (its size relative to the other elements in the space), a tile's dimensions can affect the illusion of space as much as color and pattern. Typically, smaller tiles are more appropriate for smaller spaces, lending a certain coziness that is enhanced by the greater ratio of grout lines. Larger tiles hold their own in more expansive rooms, where small tiles might look too fussy. However, in certain situations, an oversize tile can actually make a room seem larger, particularly when laid on the diagonal, which extends the illusion of space. And small tiles can lend intimacy and texture to a bland space. In a small space, using a large-size tile on the floor and a smaller coordinate on counters or walls provides continuity; and the size differential adds visual interest. Or you can mix different sizes or shapes of tiles in the same color on either floor or wall. Narrow grout lines in a color closely matched to the tile play down the individual blocks and enhance spaciousness. Another visual trick is to run rectangular tiles across the floor of a narrow room or hallway, making a con-

fining space seem wider. Here are some other spatial design tricks to ponder:

• To expand a space, use the same tiles on floors and walls—perhaps in different sizes. The continuity avoids any busyness that creates a sense of confinement.

• To focus attention on a particular area or to create a subtle pattern, alternate shapes of the same tile. In a kitchen with a breakfast bay, square pavers in the work area could shift to hexagonal pavers bordered by squares to define the eating area and accentuate its angled walls.

• Use a smaller version of a tile in a small adjoining space. A kitchen might feature 8-inch square tiles; in the adjacent pantry and laundry room, the scale could switch to 6 inches. Or run the tile on the diagonal in the kitchen, with a transition to a right-angled approach in an adjoining family room.

• A herringbone or other angled design alleviates the straight lines that can cramp small spaces.

• Two related colors of the same tile set horizontally on the wall could similarly make a tight bathroom "read" larger.

## BORDER PATROL

One of the most exciting aspects of tile design lies in the use of specialty borders. As soon as tile became a decorative surface as well as simply a building material that offered protection from dampness and the extremes of climate, border treatments appeared on the scene. They were integral to Egyptian tile makers, who were adept at using squares, diamonds, and triangles to create zigzags and other geometric repetitions. Naturalistic motifs such as lotus blossoms also originated with the Egyptians; waves, ropes, fish, dolphins, starfish, and shell motifs came from Minoan Crete and other ancient seafaring cultures. Many classical designs were handed down to the Greeks and Romans, and then resurrected during the Renaissance. Some sport such evocative names as Vitruvian scroll and guilloche. Others, like the Egyptian ziggurat or the Greek key, look remarkably contemporary.

Borders come painted, in relief, or simply in a coordinated or contrasting color to field tile. You needn't limit yourself to one border tile. Layering two or three borders or interspersing them within rows of field tile can create enormous visual excitement.

The most common use of a wall border is to terminate the tile where it meets another surface. At the base of the wall or at the ceiling, it acknowledges the transition to another plane. But don't stop there. Create a chair rail or dado with a border tile, or install a border at picture-rail height. Frame a mirror or go up and around doorways and windows. Borders can create

**OPPOSITE:** Designer Diane Provenzano tiled a bathroom dado in inexpensive factory-made earth-tone tile, then added interest with a border of ceramic mosaics in crisp black and white. The plaster wall above was tinted to match the tile. **BELOW:** Proving that neutral can be dramatic, the floor in this New Mexico foyer was copied from one in a house in France. Instead of executing the pattern in marble, Mexican terra-cotta tiles were stained in four shades, ranging from white to dark brown, then sealed with a penetrating finish.

architectural interest where there is none, accentuate good features, or disguise an eyesore like two different ceiling heights. They can bracket a mural or define the transition on a wall from one field tile to another or from right-angle to diagonal tile placement. A well-designed border should not interrupt an established horizontal line by dead-ending. Instead, it should be manipulated to turn a corner or go up or down before resuming its original height. (See chapter 3, On the Floor, for more on floor borders.)

When using tiles of different sizes, recognize that the joints will probably not line up. In such cases, it's generally better to exaggerate the difference rather than attempt to line the joints up. Traditionally, grout lines of borders are offset from those of field tile, to enhance the border's role as a framing device.

Not all borders are made with accent tiles. Without using expensive trim pieces, different field tiles can do the trick. For example, surround a classic black-and-white checkerboard field with a row of black, a row of white, and a final row that echoes the central pattern. Create borders by exploiting the following concepts:

• Vary the shape. For example, frame square tiles with brick-shaped ones.

• Vary the size. Contain a field of large squares with smaller squares.

• Vary the color. A border of deep green glazed squares sets off terra cotta beautifully.

• Vary the placement. Switch from end-to-end alignment to staggered or angled.

• Add pattern. A border of decorated tile one tile deep enlivens a solid-color field.

**OPPOSITE:** A border of Tunisian tile delineates the painted wainscot and baseboards of a covered patio at Casa del Herrero in Montecito, California. **ABOVE:** Blue Slide Art Tile's relief fish tiles, topped with tiny mosaics and an ogee molding, form a complex border in an otherwise simple white bathroom.

## MAKING TRADE-OFFS

If you're not working with an unlimited budget, you'll want to think carefully about where to make the biggest investment. You can always go for quality over quantity by investing in a smashing specialty tile as a border for a simple field tile. Your eye will be more drawn to an unusual tile when it appears as an accent than when it is used everywhere. Be sure to place the specialty tile where it will have the greatest impact. Since you see vertical surfaces before horizontal ones, splurge on a wonderful tile for a backsplash area rather than choose a costly floor tile. Or highlight expensive handmade tiles as a center design surrounded by more moderately priced factory-made ones. Another budget-conscious idea is to purchase second-grade floor tile, which has passed all technical requirements but may have some minor defects in appearance. You can also use inexpensive factory-made tiles for these high-impact looks:

- Arrange squares in a variety of solid colors to create a striped, plaid, or basketweave pattern, perhaps as a "runner" in a hallway.
- "Hang" a patchwork quilt formed of solid-color tile in squares and triangles on a shower or bathtub wall.
- Use a solid-color field tile, then design a border using two or more coordinated colors. If you want to get a little bolder, cut the squares into halves to form triangles.
- Purchase odd lots or closeout tiles in several colors or designs to create a one-of-a-kind pattern.
- Use an inexpensive field tile randomly or deliberately interspersed with a more expensive or hand-painted tile; or use a custom border with a stock field tile.
- Commission a mural for a key area, such as a backsplash or the long wall of a tub surround, then fill in with stock tiles.

## THE IMPORTANCE OF GROUT

The filler between tiles, grout is small in area but vast in importance, the final element that can make or break an installation. (It can also be the key to more carefree maintenance.) Grout

**LEFT:** Glaze puddled in depressions of the high-relief medieval-inspired animal motif tiles by Moore-Merkowitz heightens their three-dimensional quality.

should really be viewed as a design component. Tile manufacturers often suggest a grout width for a particular product, but within reason you can size up or down, depending on your preference. A narrow grout line focuses attention on an outstanding tile and allows an overall design to carry seamlessly from one tile to the next. Most factory-made wall tiles are precision-sized so they can be butted with grout lines as thin as $\frac{1}{16}$ inch, although the line can also be as wide as $\frac{1}{4}$ inch if you prefer. Solid-color handmade tiles often look better with a thicker grout line, perhaps up to $\frac{1}{2}$ inch, which becomes the dominant element in the pattern and also allows for slight irregularities in size. On the other hand, handmade tiles with significant color variation should be butted close together so that the grout lines do not detract from the play of hues.

Another design decision is whether to use a "full" (or "high") grout line, which is nearly flush with the surface of the tile, or a more washed-out effect, in which the grout sits just below the tile's surface. To a large degree, this decision is affected by the tile, which may have either sharp, 90-degree edges, or more rounded, relieved edges. The former, including ground-edge quarry tile, calls for a high, flat grout line flush with the surface; with handmade tiles or those with a rounded top edge, and a wider grout line, a slightly lower look can be appealing. On walls, the only considerations are type of tile and preferred look, but for floors, maintenance and safety are factors: A high, narrow line is easier to keep clean; the joint of a relieved edge is less likely to snag high-heeled shoes; and a concave style is not suitable for wet areas, where water will puddle in the joints.

Grout comes in a wide spectrum of colors. Typically, floor grout is gray, to hide dirt; white is common on walls, but for a unified look, match grout to tile color. A contrasting color, on the other hand, emphasizes the grid or other pattern formed by the tiles and can be used to dramatic effect—say, red grout with a charcoal gray tile.

A few other practical notes: Take time to test your chosen grout on a 1-foot-square tiled panel (or a larger area with a large tile). Let it dry and be sure you like the color and the thickness of the line before proceeding with the job. Check to see if crazing, the tiny hairline cracks on tile, picks up a dark or bold grout color during application. And when buying tile, advise the salesperson about the grout width you plan. In a large installation, it could make a difference in the amount of tile you will need.

**RIGHT:** Bold gray grout emphasizes the diagonal pattern of the wall tile and avoids the dilemma of changing grout color from one tile color to another.

**OPPOSITE, FROM TOP:** In compound border situations with pieces of different sizes, grout lines should be offset rather than lined up; aquamarine grout matches tile glaze. Tiles comprising a hand-painted vignette are butted closely together so that the narrow grout line does not distract from the design. Hand-molded tiles, such as these Epro hexagons, look best with a wide grout line that compensates for their irregularity. Color variation from tile to tile is accentuated by a narrow grout line in a coordinated coppery hue.

# 3

# On the Floor

*In terms of sheer volume, more tile is used for floors than for any other purpose. Floors rarely get the attention lavished on walls, but a striking tile floor can make the smallest, most architecturally uninspired room come alive. And what could be stronger underfoot? Just think of the encaustic tile floors of English churches that have served the devout for centuries. It is essential that you use only tile specified for floor use, which is tougher than that suitable only for walls. Quarry and porcelain tiles are ideal choices; terra cotta is not as hard but can be used in many interior situations. Although unglazed, all offer enormous diversity of color and style. (Some unglazed tiles do need to be sealed in certain situations. See Seal for Satisfaction, page 179.) Changes in technology have meant that where once only unglazed tiles*

were durable enough for heavy-duty use, there are now many glazed options, ranging from sleek, thin contemporary looks to thicker, more rustic ones, referred to by a variety of names.

A note on terminology: Although the words *tile* and *paver* are often used interchangeably, properly only dust-pressed floor tiles are called pavers; extruded products are known as tiles. Traditionally, pavers tended to have a rounded, irregular, or "natural" edge when viewed in profile; extruded tiles had a sharper, flatter edge.

## COMPARATIVE VIRTUES

Tile's advantages as a flooring material are unquestionable and numerous: beauty, durability, relative ease of maintenance, and environmental friendliness. In the debit column, tile can be cold on bare feet, unforgiving to dropped dishes and glasses, and tiring to stand on for hours on end. But when compared to carpet, wood, stone, or vinyl, tile affords very tangible benefits. Most tiles don't require refinishing as wood does and tile won't dent as soft woods do. Unlike carpet, it doesn't wear out quickly or harbor dust and other allergens. While vinyl and synthetic carpets may give off toxic gases, tile is a natural, stable product. And compared to stone and terrazzo, tile is easier and less expensive to install.

> I think a caveman discovered the first terra-cotta tile. It would have been after the rainy season when, bored with the inactivity of his cave, he ventured out to find that the muddy earth had, quite quickly, been turned rock hard from the heat of the sun.
> —Graham Clark, Managing Director, Fired Earth

All floor tiles are not created equal. Abrasion resistance, slip resistance, porosity, breaking strength, stain resistance, and frost resistance all affect the uses for which an individual tile is appropriate. Highly glazed tile is generally suitable only where scratching is unlikely. The same tile that performs admirably on a powder room floor could prove a disaster in heavy kitchen traffic. Likewise, a dining room where chairs are frequently scraped across the floor or an area with direct access to the outdoors will need abrasion-resistant tiles. In a room that is used infrequently or where you tend to go barefoot—like a bedroom—any floor tile will usually do the job.

In kitchens, baths, and entries, where moisture is a given, tiles with low water absorption rates and slip resistance are essential. Matte or textured glazed tile are typically specified for these areas. The most slip-resistant tiles have abrasive particles on the surface or raised ridges, dots, or another pattern. Used primarily in commercial settings, their highly textured surface may make them difficult to clean. Heavy-duty quarry tile, porcelain, and matte-glazed floor tiles are better residential options, as they can withstand tracked-in water and grit but are easily cleaned. Any tile used in a wet area should be recommended as slip-resistant by the manufacturer. (See chapters 4, 5, and 7 for more on selecting appropriate tiles for kitchens, baths, and outdoor areas.)

Floor tile divides roughly into unglazed and glazed types. The following are most commonly used for floors:

### Terra Cotta

In Italian, the words *terra cotta* translate literally as "cooked earth," although the term is also broadly used for products made in Spain, France, Italy, Portugal, Mexico, Peru, and Brazil. But to use "terra cotta" as a catchall expression is inaccurate: It does not necessarily mean "red clay" or "low fire," two common misconceptions. The term is often used loosely to suggest a decorative look. (Some Mexican terra-cotta tiles are called *tierra de Saltillos* [earth of Saltillo] from the city in Sonora where they are made, or *saltillos* for short.) Terra cotta's visceral appeal comes from its irregular, handmade look, and it has become a favorite choice for country kitchens or any rustic environment. Colors range from rusty red to pink, pale yellow, and even gray. Many terra-cotta tiles are still handmade the way they were thousands of years ago and may display such imperfections as chipped corners or finger marks. Molded in individual forms and smoothed by hand, the result is what the Spanish call *el supremo arte de la imperfección.*

Terra cotta is also made in factory settings either by mechanical molding or by extrusion. These tiles tend to be more uniform in color and shape than handmade. The surface of molded tiles can be given either a smooth or a rustic finish, but

**PREVIOUS PAGES, LEFT:** Unglazed Mexican saltillo tiles in two interlocking Provençal shapes provide a lively contrast to the brushstroke glaze and shape of the fireplace tile. **CENTER:** Unglazed tiles laid on the diagonal are bordered with smaller glazed pieces. **RIGHT:** A border design silkscreened on stone-look tile appears delicate but can stand up to heavy traffic. **THIS PAGE:** Designers Jed Johnson and Scott Cornelius arranged square and rectangular hand-molded terra-cotta tiles in a basketweave pattern on a bathroom floor, accenting the junctures with tiny multicolor glazed dots.

extruded versions will have a more uniformly smooth finish. Terra-cotta tiles are at least ½ inch thick and often twice that. Many are fired at a relatively low temperature, making them unsuitable for exterior use, as they would absorb water and crack under freezing conditions. (See chapter 7, The Great Outdoors, for information on outdoor use of terra cotta.)

Terra-cotta tiles come in numerous shapes and sizes. They can also be glazed, and although not a good choice for a whole floor, work well as colorful accents against an unglazed field. Terra cotta can also be hand-painted, decorated with a stenciled white glaze, or incised, all of which are equally effective as borders and accent pieces. Low-relief terra cotta is suitable only for walls.

There is a wide variation in both terra cotta's quality and its price that reflects not only the country of origin but also the manufacturing techniques used. Some people love the rustic charm of pockmarked surfaces and irregular edges; others prefer a smooth finish and more sharply defined edges. Check out the porosity of various products. Terra cotta can be nonvitreous or semivitreous, and is considered a special-purpose tile because it does not conform to ANSI standards set for quarry tile or pavers. Make sure the retailer knows how you want to use the tile, and follow his or her recommendations for installation and maintenance. (For information on sealing terra cotta, see Seal for Satisfaction on page 179.) For all its beauty, terra cotta often requires more care than other types of floor tile. There are numerous glazed, low-maintenance products available that offer a similar look.

European terra-cotta tiles reclaimed from renovations or demolitions of manor houses, châteaux, and barns represent the ultimate in rusticity. Most are at least a century old and some considerably more. For all their mellow appeal, antique tiles vary considerably in size and thickness, making installation tricky and expensive. Be sure you use an installer familiar with antique tile. A simpler and less costly alternative would be to use new tiles that are distressed to mimic the patina of age. Another way to achieve an antique effect is to use new tiles upside down. (If you elect to take this route, be sure to tell your supplier so you get suitable tiles.) The porous nature of terra cotta means that the color can also be modified with whitewash or other stains—just make sure that the base of the solvent and the colorant are compatible.

## Quarry Tile

Made from clay and usually shale by the extrusion process, quarry tile is extremely durable and its slightly rough texture is naturally skidproof, making it an ideal flooring for kitchens, mudrooms, and any rooms that open to the outdoors. The extrusion process forms a tough "die-skin" on all surfaces, enhancing the tile's stain resistance. Like terra cotta, the colors of shale and clay—white, brown, red, gray, and ocher—provide a range of natural hues when fired, although oxides may be added for certain hues such as blue and green. Quarry tile can have a uniform, machine-made look or a handcrafted look. Due to its higher firing temperature, it is stronger and more impervious to water than most products referred to as terra cotta. Rated as vitreous or semivitreous, quarry tile resists acids, oils, and detergents. While highly stain-resistant, it is not completely stainproof, and some manufacturers recommend that it be sealed in high-use areas, particularly pale colors.

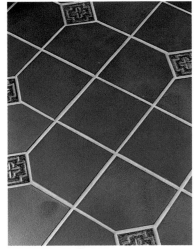

Quarry tiles range from 3 inches square to 12 inches square and also come in rectangles, hexagons, and a variety of other shapes. Thickness varies from ¼ inch to a full inch. To enliven the look of quarry tile, you can mix various hues, either in a pattern or at random, or add inserts of glazed tile. (Quarry tile itself is sometimes glazed.) Quarry tiles and other unglazed tiles may exhibit flashing, areas that randomly appear darker or lighter than others as a result of the reaction of oxides in the clay to extreme heat in the firing process. Some cheaper tiles have been chemically treated to give the appearance of flashing, but are easy to spot because the pattern will be identical instead of the random effect achieved naturally.

**ABOVE:** Metropolitan Ceramics' quarry tile is accented with glazed molded inserts, also of quarry tile. **OPPOSITE, TOP LEFT:** Original dark red terra-cotta squares frame a "rubble" mosaic floor in a 1920s Italianate house in Coral Gables. **TOP RIGHT:** Flashing on London Ceramics' handmade terra-cotta *provençals* enhances their unusual shape. **CENTER LEFT:** Antique terra cotta, complete with paw print, is bordered with new diamond-shaped pieces. **CENTER RIGHT:** Terra cotta frames a "carpet" of glazed and decorated tiles. **BOTTOM LEFT:** Large French terra-cotta squares meet smaller glazed squares in a stepped pattern laid on the diagonal. **BOTTOM RIGHT:** A beeswax finish gives French terra-cotta tiles a warm luster.

## Porcelain Tile

Porcelain is generally made from kaolin clay and feldspar (silica-based rock that has been ground), usually by the dust-pressed method. Rated as impervious, porcelain has many advantages as a floor tile, its extremely high firing temperatures making it even harder than natural stone and thereby stain- and scratch-resistant. In unglazed porcelain, the color may extend throughout the clay body. Unglazed pavers are colored with natural pigments in the form of mineral oxides that produce an array of colors, although the high firing temperature makes it impossible to get bright red.

Porcelain pavers also come in mottled terrazzo looks, and in polished, unpolished, and textured versions. Polished porcelain has the sheen of a glazed tile; since polishing opens up the pores of the tile, it is often recommended that it be sealed for floor use. The smooth, matte, unpolished finish is ideal for bathroom floors; one textured finish mimics natural slate. There are also slip-resistant designs such as grids. Equally useful as a counter tile and a wall tile, porcelain comes in 6-, 8-, and 12-inch squares and sometimes even larger, and can be cut on site easily. Since most unglazed porcelain has color all the way through the body, there are no raw edges or glaze to chip when cutting; and the relative flatness keeps the surface even when cut. Porcelain tile can also be glazed, a less expensive process than polishing, and one that makes it possible to achieve any color.

Until recently, porcelain tile has been used primarily for commercial installations, but it is becoming increasingly popular in homes. With its smooth surface, in mottled finishes porcelain can convey the formality of granite or terrazzo, at a much lower price. The marvelous color range makes it equally suited to playful designs that mimic plaids or patchwork quilts. Among its greatest virtues, its strength allows porcelain to be cut into curved as well as straight-line shapes for even greater design flexibility. Water-jet technology has made it possible to custom-order intricately cut shapes—waves, for example—as inset designs. The finished look of porcelain is complemented by the use of a thin grout line.

## Ceramic Mosaics

The classic small black and white hexagons, known as "hexies," found in baths dating from the early part of the century are termed *ceramic mosaics.* Also made in square, round (called "pennies"), and rectangular (called "chicklets") shapes and in a wide range of colors, they are popular once again, and can be used throughout the house.

Technically, mosaics are smaller than other tiles, measuring less than 6 square inches, and from $\frac{1}{4}$ to $\frac{3}{8}$ inch thick. They usually come mounted on a sheet of paper or plastic mesh for ease of installation. Porcelain mosaics are often unglazed, taking their color from the pigments in the body of the clay, and are impervious. Porcelain mosaics can also be glazed; mosaics made from other clays are always glazed. Like porcelain, they too are equally useful as wall tiles.

**LEFT:** A checkered pattern of Crossville's porcelain tile takes on an added dimension with star shapes cut by water-jet technology. **OPPOSITE:** In a hallway between two rooms a narrow accent of colorful ceramic mosaics alludes to the pattern in the far room, where mosaics and terra cotta are partners in a basketweave pattern. Door frames are marked with rectangular tiles laid on the horizontal.

## Alleviating the Chill

If a tile floor is to be part of a major remodeling or addition, consider installing radiant heating in the cement sub-floor. Heated electric coils or flexible tubing filled with water radiate warmth through the tile to warm the whole room. Where once costly copper was used as tubing, today plastic tubing makes radiant floor heating more cost competitive with conventional systems; any initial higher cost may be amortized by lower heating bills. A less costly alternative? Well-placed area rugs or a warm pair of socks or slippers.

Thanks to their small size, mosaics encourage creative use in geometric designs. If sufficient quantities are ordered, several manufacturers will make up custom designs on mesh. Ceramic mosaics are not to be confused with glass mosaics, which are often composed on site of even smaller pieces.

## Glazed Floor Tile

The term *glazed floor tile* lumps together tiles with a wide range of looks: They may be hand molded or machine made, red or white bodied. The ability to glaze a "green" (unfired) tile has been around for decades; the glaze actually fuses with the clay body. Today tile manufacturers in the United States, Italy, Mexico, and other countries use machinery that allows the bisque and glazing processes to take place simultaneously in a single trip through an extremely high temperature kiln. Because the tiles can be spray-dried, pressed, dried again, glazed, fired, and boxed in a very short period of time, manufacturing costs—

and prices to the consumer—are lower. (The Italians call this dust-pressed process—and the tiles made this way—*monocottura,* meaning "single firing.") Glazed floor tiles come in solid colors, textures, and designs, including complex looks such as plaids. Finishes may be matte, semi-gloss, or glossy. Thanks to its affordability, variety of colors, and easy maintenance, glazed floor tile is now the favorite choice for kitchens. It does not require sealing and needs only regular sweeping or vacuuming and removal of spills.

Vitrified glazed floor tiles are extremely hard and abrasion-resistant, making them an ideal flooring for areas where tracked-in sand and dirt would scratch other tiles. They work well on most interior floors and some exterior applications.

Glazed quarry tile is another handsome option. The tiles are glazed after being extruded and are also made by a single-firing process. The term *glazed stoneware* refers to a thicker and more rustic-looking product than glazed floor tiles, and is considered

a special-purpose tile. Such tiles range from ½ to ¾ inch thick and come in 4- to 12-inch squares as well as numerous other shapes. Glazed stoneware often has a handcrafted look, even when made in a factory setting. It may have a red or a white clay body and comes in a marvelous array of glaze colors. Small insets of glazed stoneware can be a stunning accent on terra-cotta or quarry tile floors. Some glazed tiles can withstand freezing and thawing cycles and thus successfully bridge indoor-outdoor installations. Check the manufacturer's recommendations.

Some glazed earthenware, whiteware, and other so-called special-purpose tiles can be used for floors in special, low-traffic situations. Or insets or borders of such materials can accent more durable floor tile.

## *Encaustic Tiles*

Another special-purpose tile, encaustic tiles are unglazed and derive their design from the use of two or more contrasting color clays. Tremendously popular in the Victorian era—they pave the floors in the United States Capitol, the Smithsonian Institution, and many state government buildings—these tiles are enjoying a revival today. Their forebears originated in monastic potteries in twelfth-century Britain, where the industry flourished until the Reformation resulted in the closing of all monasteries. Although the tiles survived on the church floors, the art of making them was forgotten. It was not until

1830 that the English revived the craft, impressing a pattern into a flat slab of clay and then filling the indentation with a contrasting-color clay in liquid form, known as slip. After the composite tile dries, it is scraped clean and flat before firing. The term *encaustic* refers to the burning in of the pattern in the firing process. Encaustic tiles always have a flat, graphic look that distinguishes them from surface-decorated designs.

Today true encaustic ceramic tiles are made in quantity by only a few companies, primarily in Great Britain. Most designs are traditional in look and are often used in historic restorations. After plastic clay is pressed into a mold, it gradually contracts; it is then removed, and the indentations are carefully filled with liquid clay

## Cement Copies

Some cement tiles mimic the look of ceramic. The impostors pretend to be terra cotta or stoneware by using tinted cement that is poured into molds, then laid like tile. Another method involves pouring cement on site and scoring it to resemble individual tiles. In both cases portland cement is used as grout. More finished looks are achieved by tinting molded cement tiles with swirls of color to suggest marble or granite and then pressing them under extreme weight for a fine-grained, durable body, which can then be enhanced with polish. Another type, called mission tiles or loosely referred to as encaustic tiles, made in Mexico, Morocco, and Malta, resemble true encaustic tiles in that different colors of cement are used to form designs that penetrate the body of the tile. But unlike the real thing, cement tiles are not fired and the design is not burned in. They are weight-pressed for strength and a smooth finish. Some mix in marble dust for added strength. Cement tiles are porous and subject to stains, and the body is not as strong as most ceramic tiles, but they are relatively inexpensive.

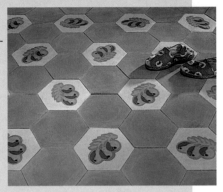

mixed with oxides to form different colors. When fired, the different clay bodies fuse together. The entire process takes many weeks, which helps explain the high cost. Tiles are typically ½ inch thick with an inlaid design 1/16 inch deep. (Makers also offer solid-color tiles to coordinate with patterned tiles.) Encaustic tiles will develop a slightly aged, antique look over time, with white taking on the look of marble or stone. Usually vitreous or semivitreous and sold unsealed, encaustic tiles may need to be finished with a penetrating sealer to prevent stains.

**OPPOSITE:** Reproduced by Paris Ceramics from the fourteenth-century tiles on the pope's bedroom floor in the Palace of the Popes in Avignon, these glazed and hand-painted pieces look surprisingly contemporary. **LEFT:** Hand-molded in a variety of clay colors, encaustic tiles from Country Floors and made in Italy recall Victorian designs. **ABOVE:** Based on the woodblock-print fabrics popularized by the French firm of Souleiado, these hexagonal tiles are made of cast, pressed cement. The design is achieved by using metal stencils to separate different colors of wet cement.

**PRECEDING PAGES:** This fool-the-eye Oriental rug made in the late 1920s by Malibu Potteries was painted onto bisqued terra-cotta tile using an oil-resist method to keep glazes from running into each other when refired. **ABOVE:** In a children's bathroom, designer Van-Martin Rowe designated the room's center with a hand-painted tile, then surrounded it with an argyle design in four glazed colors. **OPPOSITE, ABOVE:** Hand-painted tiles based on traditional North African designs form a runner in a field of solid-color glazed squares. Related patterns continue up the walls. **OPPOSITE, RIGHT:** On a more subtle note, terra-cotta lozenges frame limestone squares centered on a glazed ceramic insert.

## COLOR UNDERFOOT

While floor tile offers enormous color choice, in practical terms there are specific considerations: Extremely light colors show dirt more than middle tones; black, navy blue, and other dark colors can show dust and footprints; and any solid color is harder to keep looking clean than tiles with a textured or mottled effect. A general rule of thumb is that the floor should ground a room with a darker hue than that used on walls. However, this is not a hard-and-fast rule. For example, a kitchen with dark cherry cabinets could be brightened up with a lighter tile floor; celadon green tile used on a bathroom floor could keep cobalt blue walls from overwhelming a small space.

When it comes to designing patterned floors, tile is a natural. Two or more colors can be combined to create an overall pattern, such as a checkerboard or herringbone. Or separate areas within a room or an open living space can be defined by a change in color or the use of a bold border.

**ABOVE:** A myriad of shapes and sizes of Malibu tile gracefully negotiates a corner and ascends a flight of stairs at Adamson House. **RIGHT:** Mosaic "doormats" of broken tile were common in the 1920s and 1930s. Their use can be traced to an ancient belief that evil spirits could not cross such a barrier. In a 1927 Mexican Colonial house, artist Nancy Kintisch mixed original Malibu tiles with contemporary products.

## SIZE AND SHAPE

Floor tile ranges in size from less than 1 inch square to 24-inch squares and even larger, with 6-, 8-, 10-, and 12-inch squares being the norm. So-called square tiles may actually have rounded corners or rippled edges; and some factory-made tiles are molded to imitate a handmade look. Sharp 90-degree corners give a crisp, formal look to a floor, while rounded corners suggest a rustic, casual air. Most floor tiles are nominally flat; avoid the slight unevenness of pillowed tiles in rooms where you stand a lot or where dirt might collect in recessed grout lines.

While square tile is the most common and the easiest to work with, other shapes offer fascinating design possibilities. Some tiles also come in delightfully intricate shapes with equally wonderful names: ogee, or Provençal; triple *tomettes* (formed from a trio of hexagons); lozenge or navette (an elongated hexagon); and even Byzantine eight-pointed stars. Most shapes are interlocking and can be arranged in more than one pattern, sometimes forming a complex pattern with another shape, like an M. C. Escher woodcut. Two or more shapes can be combined into almost endless combinations.

## MAKING TRANSITIONS

It is important to view any floor pattern in relationship to other elements in the space. Think about the colors and designs of other surfaces in the room and, if the house has an open plan, the floors in adjoining spaces. Try to avoid jarring changes in tone and style of tile from one area to the next. For example, rough terra cotta butting up against precise porcelain pavers could strike a discordant note. But well thought out changes from space to space add interest. Consider the following:

• A pattern of large octagonal and small square terra-cotta tiles used in a country-style kitchen could travel into the more formal dining room, where the squares become glazed insets, accented by a border of similar glazed tiles.

• A contemporary open-plan house might use the same 12-inch glazed square laid on the diagonal in the kitchen and as a grid in the family room.

• A checkerboard of gray and cream tiles in a center hall could lead to a field of cream in the dining room, bordered by gray and the reverse in the living room opposite it.

• The pale blue and red tile floor in a children's shared bathroom could relate to a bedroom with a blue color scheme on one side and a red scheme on the other.

In rooms where tile is applied to another area as well as floors, pay careful attention to the spirit of the two. Look at color and scale. Does one fight with the other or is there a pleasing compatibility? Is one handmade with a rustic informality and the other a hard-edge contemporary design? It is not impossible to pull off such dramatic contrasts, but be aware of what you are doing. How will you handle the juncture where the two tiles meet? Should the floor tile climb the wall to form a baseboard? (Most floor tiles come with matching cove-base or bullnose trim.) Should the tile used on the wall reappear as an accent on the floor? Only after such questions have been successfully resolved should you order your tile.

The larger the floor, the more carefully one should plan a bold design. Entries, sunrooms, and dining rooms provide ideal locations for showstopping effects. Because most kitchen and bathroom floors are interrupted by cabinets and fixtures, they may not be the best places for ambitious designs. Instead, it might be better to use a patterned tile "bath mat" in front of a tub or a "runner" under a breakfast table. If you plan to use area rugs over a tile floor, you will probably want to stay with a simple design or a border treatment. (Turn to Pattern Play on page 170 for some classic floor patterns and border treatments.)

## ON THE BORDER

A border is one way to use tile dramatically but with more adaptability than an elaborate overall pattern allows. Like a frame that surrounds a work of art, a border lends crispness to any pattern and contributes a finishing touch. It also eases transitions, whether from floor to wall, room to room, or area to area. A border can create an entry in a living room that opens right off the front door, define a breakfast area in a large kitchen, and generally manipulate the eye to perceive any space in a favorable light. In fact, a border

**OPPOSITE:** Mosaic artist Luciano defined the eating area of an open-plan kitchen by designing a rug made of squares, rectangles, and triangles of cement tile. In the kitchen proper, the decorative treatment is confined to a border. **LEFT:** Rectangles and large squares contain small solid color tiles.

should be avoided only in irregular spaces where it would exaggerate any oddness or in an area so small that the relationship between border and field cannot be clearly established.

Perhaps the simplest border treatment is to lay the tiles used in the main area in a different way—squares laid diagonally as the field bounded by squares set end to end, for example. Another subtle but effective way to add architectural interest to any room is to use a border of a different shape in the same finish. Each change of direction, shape, or color adds to the possibilities. For instance, you could, in increasing degrees of complexity:

- Border squares with a row of rectangles.
- Double up with two rows of rectangles.
- Lay the squares on the diagonal. Where the field meets the border, every other square tile will have to be cut into a triangle, creating a double border.
- Enclose the rectangles in a third border of squares running flush with the perimeter of the room.
- Use two different colors for the diagonally laid square field tiles, creating a checkerboard effect.

When different colors and surface designs are added to

the equation, border possibilities are limitless. Although some designs are made specifically as borders, virtually any flat tile can be used. A highly glazed decorative tile can serve as a dramatic border in contrast to unglazed or matte-finish field tile. Other border ideas:

- Play off unpolished porcelain pavers against a border of the same color in a polished finish, for subtle contrast.
- Frame a terra-cotta floor with a border of terra-cotta tile decorated with a stenciled or silk-screen glaze.
- Run a border of tumbled granite and marble mosaics beside a quarry tile field.
- Ring porcelain pavers with 1-inch ceramic mosaics in a Greek key design.
- Enliven a neutral field tile with a glass mosaic border (sold in preformed sheets).

## MIXED MEDIA

Recent years have seen an increased popularity of limestone, slate, and tumbled marble and granite tiles. Although they can be expensive on their own, used in combination with ceramic tile all are more affordable. The stone may be a small accent—maybe a medallion of black slate used with a rosy red octagonal ceramic tile—or the tile may play the supporting role, perhaps as a border to a limestone floor. Terrazzo, a conglomeration of marble chips embedded in a cement or resin base and then polished, may also be combined with ceramic tile to interesting effect. For centuries Europeans have framed squares of tile in bands of hardwood. A simpler treatment is to border a tile floor with strips or planks of wood or reverse the combination and enliven a wood floor with a frame of tile. Such a treatment gracefully handles the transition from a tile kitchen floor to wood in a nearby dining room. When mixing tiles in a border treatment, whether all ceramic or a mix with stone or glass, be sure thicknesses are uniform, or your installer will have to compensate for any variation.

**ABOVE LEFT:** Brick pavers enclose a trompe l'oeil rug, its pattern formed of squares and elongated hexagons. **OPPOSITE:** Made of shaped ceramic tile, a salmon leaps through a mosaic river of green slate and tiny tile squares. **OVERLEAF, LEFT:** Venetian glass mosaics, plus a few glass droplets, create a jewel-like surface on the floor of a tiny powder room. **RIGHT:** A tile mural of shimmering fish by Architectural Accents makes an instantaneous impact in the entry of a Colorado house.

# 4

# In the Kitchen

*The kitchen has been the traditional showcase for tile. Dutch, French, Spanish, Portuguese, and Mexican kitchens dating back to the eighteenth and nineteenth centuries displayed an exuberant use of tile. Almost altars to food, these rooms often mixed several colors and patterns, with tiles stretching across counters and climbing walls—sometimes even onto the ceilings.*

*Like any classic material, tile works well in kitchens of all styles, whether clean-lined contemporary, low-key traditional, Arts and Crafts revival, or all-out country charming. In fact, the newest look in kitchens reflects not a particular style, but an eclecticism that deftly mixes styles, colors, and materials. So instead of thinking in either-or terms, consider blending ceramic tile with granite, wood, stainless steel, solid surfacing (the generic term for Corian,*

Gibraltar, Avonite, and the like), and other materials. The play of textures and colors can add interest, warmth, and personality to the room that is the heart of most homes.

As legions of restaurant kitchens show, tile is the chef's material of choice not just for its decorative qualities, but for its practical virtues. Durable, fireproof, water- and usually stain-resistant, hygienic, and easy to keep clean, ceramic tile satisfies the workhorse demands of any kitchen. In today's increasingly high-tech kitchens, tile also fulfills an important role, adding warmth and personality to spaces that can all too easily become sterile. Happily, in its infinite variety, tile works as beautifully in a country-style kitchen as it does in a sleek contemporary setting. Whether cladding a ventilation hood, surrounding a commercial range, or framing an over-the-sink window and sill, tile is always at home in the kitchen.

While tile can be an important element in kitchen design, it must be considered in conjunction with other surfaces. This principle of design applies to any material and cannot be stated too often. The most beautiful tile in the world won't look good if it is competing for attention with several other components of equal weight. When thinking about tile color, remember that your choice may have an impact on the lighting in the room. A large expanse of a dark color will absorb light, requiring compensation with natural and artificial light. Remember also that the kitchen is first and foremost a place to prepare and serve meals. There is no doubt that certain colors offer a more appealing backdrop for food than others.

## FLOOR ESSENTIALS

As discussed in chapter 3, On the Floor, a ceramic tile kitchen floor does have some drawbacks, as does any flooring material. Tile can be cold underfoot. It is less forgiving on the legs than more resilient materials and likewise will not spare plates and glasses dropped on it. But without a doubt, tile is practical, long lasting, and easy to keep clean. It is more durable and more water-resistant than wood and more attractive and permanent than vinyl. If you spend a lot of time cooking, you may want to use rugs or mats in front of the range and sink to add a measure of comfort.

> **Put your money into the back-splash. It's the first thing you see when you walk into a kitchen.**
>
> —Gail Green, Interior Designer

A few practical considerations also bear repeating with respect to selecting floor tile for your kitchen. Check with the salesperson to be sure the tile is appropriate for this use. Choose a product that is slip-resistant when wet. Most terra cotta must be sealed for kitchen use or it will stain when grease and other foods are spilled on it; some people seal quarry tile and other unglazed tile as well. (See Seal for Satisfaction, page 179.) White or other pale hues will show dirt more readily, as will extremely dark colors. Heavily textured or pillowed tile will collect dirt and should be avoided in kitchens. Pass up any tiles that are extremely uneven. If your feet aren't firmly flat on the floor, you will tire more quickly. In other words, comfort and health should not be sacrificed to a "look."

## Crucial Tolerances

Installing tile will raise the height of a floor slightly, which may have an impact on adjoining rooms, requiring that new doorsills be laid once a tile floor is installed. Existing doors will usually have to be planed down and rehung. When laying a new kitchen floor, you'll have to decide whether to tile under all the appliances or up to them. The former is preferable, but it will raise the height of the appliances slightly, which could create a problem with a slide-in stove or built-in dishwasher (if you are not planning to install new counters also). If you opt to tile up to the edge of the appliances rather than under them, be sure that you are not raising the floor to a height that makes it impossible to slide them out for repair. Drop-in stoves and built-in ovens will not present any difficulties, but slide-in ranges, dishwashers, washing machines, and clothes dryers do require a margin of space for access. In a complete remodeling, it is best to tile under where the appliances will be installed to protect the substrate from leaks.

**PREVIOUS PAGES, LEFT:** Translucent glazes on reproductions of English Victorian tiles, used here as a backsplash, reveal delicate relief designs. **CENTER:** Under-cabinet lighting highlights the crackle glaze of reproduction delft tiles. **RIGHT:** *Culinarios* are a perennial kitchen favorite. **OPPOSITE:** Based on a traditional patchwork pattern, "Sailboat," a single graphic design by Native Tile, is rotated in different directions to form a dramatic floor quilt in an otherwise vintage kitchen.

**ABOVE:** Around the window recess in a Manhattan kitchen, skillful cuts turn the corner without interrupting the flow of the design. Bullnose trim gives an equally neat finish to the windowsill. **RIGHT:** A backsplash depicting the birds of Central Park—grosbeaks, tanningers, and blue jays—by Blue Slide Art Tile brings a breath of fresh air to the room.

## Accentuate the Positive

Here are some tile accent ideas for kitchens:
• Tile the top on an existing kitchen table or use a sheet of exterior-grade plywood and attach wooden legs or set it in a wrought iron base.
• Tile a kitchen fireplace or one in an adjoining room in a design compatible with the backsplash tile.
• Add a tiled shelf or niche to hold utensils behind a cooktop or range.
• A shallow, narrow niche between studs can be tiled, then fitted with glass shelves for spices and condiments.
• Tile the niche below a built-in cooktop and fit it with stainless "Metro" shelves to store pots and pans.
• Tile between ceiling beams in a country kitchen.
• Update simple wooden cabinet doors with a quartet of tiles, placed on the diagonal and framed with molding.
• Tile all four sides of a pass-through between kitchen and dining area.
• Accent a tray, or dropped, ceiling over a dining area with a tile border.
• Insert a few tiles into a solid-surfacing counter for decorative interest or near the range in a butcher block or laminate counter as a set-down area for hot pots.

Kitchen floors lend themselves to all sorts of designs; the key is to remember that the floor is only one component in the whole scheme. A bold pattern in two contrasting colors will draw the eye to the floor. In a contemporary kitchen with unadorned, flat surfaces elsewhere, you may want the floor to play the starring role, perhaps with a special treatment highlighting the sink, range, or breakfast area. If, on the other hand, you want your cabinets or a backsplash to be the focal point, you may choose to play down the floor, perhaps concentrating on a handsome perimeter design instead of an overall pattern.

Give careful attention to the shape of your kitchen, not only the actual dimensions of the room but also the floor space that is created by the cabinets and appliances. If the space is broken up, perhaps by a dining peninsula that juts into the room, a simple treatment is preferable to a complex pattern or one with a border. However, if the cabinets are installed on an angle, you could emphasize their placement with a border treatment that follows the same angle. A narrow galley kitchen might benefit from a dramatic floor design, such as one that mimics an Oriental rug or a diagonal basketweave. In general, diagonal placement seems to expand small spaces visually.

To integrate the floor with the rest of the room, consider repeating an element that appears elsewhere. Reprise a Malibu tile backsplash with smaller versions set into the corners of solid-color octagons. Or refer to a granite counter with a tumbled granite tile border banding a ceramic tile floor.

One of the hallmarks of good architectural design is the graceful transition from one plane to another or from one material to another. When tiling a kitchen floor, by all means tile the toe kick area, which takes constant abuse and is one of the first vertical planes one sees when entering a room. In fact, some interior designers believe that this area is second only to the backsplash in terms of importance. When floor and toe kick use the same tile, the cabinets appear to float over the floor, giving a pleasing continuity. If your budget is limited, consider using tile on the toe kick even if it can't be used on the floor.

## On the Counter

The matter of using tile on countertops provokes a lively dialogue. In areas where tile has a strong heritage, its use is common.

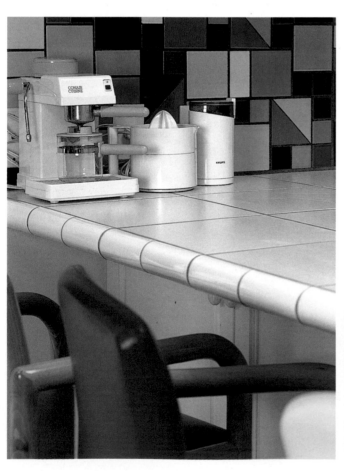

## Handle with Care

To ensure that tile kitchen counters perform well for years, establish a few family rules:

• Never use tile as a cutting surface. Knives may damage the glaze and the hardness of the tile may dull the blade's edge. Instead, inset a wooden cutting board in the tile surface. Or buy a freestanding board—and keep it out so it will be used at all times!

• Clean up all spills immediately.

• Avoid leaving out wine glasses that could spill on tiles. Red wine can stain and all wines are acidic. (Acids, including fruit juices, etch and eventually damage some tiles. They may also cause cementitious grouts to deteriorate and can discolor tinted grouts.)

• Be careful when plunking down heavy casserole dishes, which could crack tiles. Remember to be gentle or use trivets.

• Never clean tile with abrasive cleaners or those containing acid, bleach, or even a solution of white vinegar and water without checking manufacturer's instructions first. (Also see Ongoing Maintenance, page 180.)

But many designers and homeowners feel that because food can collect in joints and proper maintenance is necessary to keep grout in good shape, tile is a less appealing alternative than granite, solid surfacing, wood, or laminate. Unlike these other materials, tile is not perfectly even and flat. You certainly would not want to roll out a piecrust on a tile counter.

Fortunately, if you like the look of tile, there are ways to overcome its drawbacks. The use of 100 percent solid epoxy grout (rather than a cement-based product) can eliminate maintenance headaches. Using a large tile, such as two rows of 12-inch squares or even a single row of 24-inch ones with relatively few joints, avoids some of the disadvantages of a tile counter. Or use tile on selected counters, topping at least one work area with solid surfacing, stone, or laminate. You might confine tile to one place, say around the cooktop or the sink.

**OPPOSITE, LEFT:** Half-round trim completes a white-tiled counter that is an excellent foil to the multicolor backsplash. **OPPOSITE, RIGHT:** Bullnose trim gives a clean line to the edges of this crystalline glaze tile counter. **ABOVE LEFT:** Wine label decals fired onto tile make an appropriate surface for a wet bar, which is finished with wood trim. **ABOVE RIGHT:** A checkerboard counter is finished with V-cap edge trim.

**OPPOSITE:** Designer Beverly Ellsley used a pastiche of antique English Victorian transferware tiles on a kitchen backsplash and island. **ABOVE:** On the massive island, a core of tile serves a decorative purpose, framed by a working surface of granite slabs.

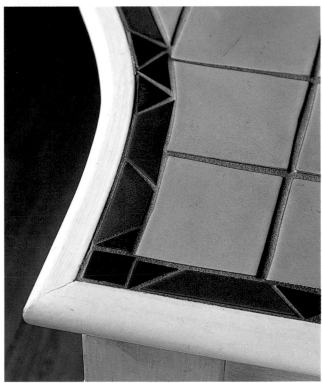

**LEFT:** Tiles by Brenda Bertin proved the inspiration for the painted finish on this kitchen's cabinets. Around the range, a checkerboard of tile provides a fireproof surface. **TOP:** Insets of Portuguese tiles depicting rural scenes acknowledge the island's change in level. **ABOVE:** Counters are bordered in Bertin's small multicolor tiles, then embraced by curved wood molding.

**ABOVE:** Architects Harry Elson and Jason Gold used tiny, inconspicuous incandescent lights mounted beneath overhead cabinets so as not to distort the colors of tile. In the glass-shelved tiled niche, recessed can lights were used to accentuate the irregularity of the tile's lustrous glaze.

## Lighting Pointers

Before finalizing a backsplash design, consider how undercabinet lighting will be handled. Avoid large light fixtures that are visible at eye level. And stay away from standard fluorescent bulbs, which give a greenish cast to their surroundings and detract from the tile's natural colors. Strips of tiny incandescent or daylight-fluorescent bulbs can be hung behind the cabinet front, or reveal. The mechanism can be concealed and the warm light will not add a cast to the colors in the tile. On larger expanses of glazed tile walls the Tile Council of America recommends avoiding ceiling-mounted "wall washer" lights, which can create annoying glare and exaggerate surface variations in the tile.

Another option is to frame laminate with a tile edging.

Remember that handmade tiles are often not level enough to be practical for use on an entire counter surface. And be sure to use tile rated for countertop wear, rather than a glossy one, which can get scratched with heavy use. Either glazed tiles or unpolished porcelain tiles work well on counters, although porcelain mosaics may be too rough and the numerous grout lines can be difficult to keep clean. Dark high-gloss colors are most apt to show scratches and wear. A tile that can be laid with a thin grout line is usually preferable for maintenance reasons.

Whether you use a tile edge treatment or frame the tile in solid surfacing, wood, or metal is a matter of personal taste and regional practice. Some people find the grouted joints on a counter edge visually disturbing; others prefer it to a change in material. A complete countertop tile treatment with a V-cap or bullnose edge can use a coordinated tile or one in a contrasting color. No-drip, or V-cap, edging slopes up slightly on the front two inches of the counter to contain spills, but has a rather hefty look that some people find displeasing. Avoid mitering tiles for counter edges; they are prone to chipping in this high-use situation. Also consider that any wood used as a frame for tile will expand and contract with changes in humidity and may wick moisture into the substrate beneath the tile.

If you do opt for tile on the counter, be sure to use grout formulated to prevent staining and discourage the growth of bacteria. In the end, your decision will come down to aesthetics and whether or not you are willing to maintain the grout. To put the maintenance issue in perspective, realize that no material is a perfect counter surface, but properly installed, ceramic tile comes close. Granite and solid surfacing are extremely expensive to purchase and install, and the latter has a synthetic look that may seem out of place in certain decors. Marble is too porous and prone to stains to be useful on working surfaces. Laminate can scratch, may

delaminate, and cannot be subjected to hot pots. Butcher block stains and scratches and some people consider it unsanitary.

When tile is used around a drop-in cooktop or a sink, the installer must plan the placement carefully. Ideally, there should be no narrow pieces of tile that could break easily. Whole tiles should be used on either side of the sink, since this area has high visibility. With most stainless steel sinks, the lip of the sink will sit over the tile, hiding the edges. This is also the case with most porcelain- or enamel-glazed sinks, but you can specify a unit designed to be installed flush to the tile with grout for a smooth line. Undermount sinks can also be used with tile counters, but they require precision in cutting curved trim pieces and grouting evenly.

## BACKSPLASH AREA

As the first surface you see when you enter a kitchen, the backsplash deserves special attention. This area defines the separation between upper and lower cabinets and is usually about 18 inches high. Behind the sink, where a window may mean fewer courses of tile, a backsplash protects the wall

**ABOVE:** Laid in groups of four, tiles in eight colors on the backsplash prove a bold partner to the owner's art pottery collection. The owner selected tiles from Pewabic Pottery to recall those used in her childhood house. Dark green cabinets and stove and pale green painted walls were matched to two of the glazes.

**TOP ROW, FROM LEFT:** An elaborate pattern like this free-form tile mosaic is ideally suited to use on a shallow area. The same white crackle-glaze tile used on counters gets a decorative border on the backsplash. Sculptured and realistically painted, this mosaic mural by Architectural Accents suggests a woodland garden. A backsplash of mold-pressed tiles from Moravian Pottery & Tile Works depicts the history of the American continent; additional tiles were applied with epoxy to the stainless steel heat shield over the range. **CENTER ROW, FROM LEFT:** A shallow niche tiled in a related design to that used for the rest of the backsplash makes use of space often wasted behind a sink. A hand-painted topiary design is one of several inserted into contrasting field tile. A pair of roosters strut their stuff on factory-made bisque blanks decorated by Veva Crozier. **BOTTOM ROW, FROM LEFT:** Metallic glazed tiles echo the tones of the steel range hood; likewise, their geometric design is repeated in the pattern of the mesh filling the upper cabinet doors. A cheery potpourri of Mexican tiles is right at home in a French country kitchen. Behind a grill on a covered patio, a boldly tiled wall reaches almost to the ceiling, serving aesthetic as well as practical needs. Portuguese hand-painted tiles used as the countertop step up the wall to form a shelf, then proceed to the backsplash area.

**Opposite:** Portuguese hand-painted tiles that evoke the sixteenth century have become a classic treatment in kitchens around the world. Here, designer Fernando Sanchez used multiple designs to make a new house look centuries old. Plain white and patterned tiles with twin borders reach eight feet up the wall; behind the range, panels depict strings of vegetables. **Above:** Counters are clad in a coordinated sponged design laid on the diagonal. **Below:** Tag tiles—labeled in French—that slot into drawer fronts can also be used as borders.

from water; behind and beside a cooktop or range, it is both a fire-proof surface and one that resists the buildup of grease. In fact, codes concerning the installation of restaurant-type ranges and grills require that the immediate surrounding surfaces be fire-proof. (You may want to tile the ceiling above a commercial range as well.)

Along with practicality, a backsplash also provides a superb canvas for decoration. If this is the only surface you are tiling, you can use any ceramic product that appeals to you as long as it relates to the other colors and materials in the room. Here is the place to install a hand-painted mural, a wonderful copper-luster tile, or an intricate pattern. (Relief tiles may require more maintenance.) If you are using tile on both counter and back-splash, give thought to whether you want a uniform look or whether you prefer a contrast between the two planes. If you have a large tiled area, even a small change, such as a shift in size or shape, a border, or an inset of some sort, will add interest. If you are using a back-splash all the way around the room, feel free to vary the design slightly in different areas. For example, you could switch from a solid color

to a pattern using several colors, or use different hues to define different areas. If tile is used on more than one wall, pay careful attention to your transitions. Try to avoid dead-ending a border treatment in a corner or at the end of a wall if the motif reappears elsewhere in the room; a connected design will be much more effective.

## FULL-DRESS TREATMENT

At the turn of the last century, a Victorian obsession with cleanliness inspired tile treatments that extended all the way up the kitchen wall to the ceiling. With the revival of interest in that era's white rectangular tiles, fully tiled kitchen walls are back in vogue. This treatment can be equally effective in other solid colors and shapes and gives the room a sleek, neat look by minimizing the transitions from one material to another. Likewise, eliminating the need to use wood windowsills and surrounds has a practical value. Tiling to the ceiling works best in rooms without an unrelieved expanse of tile; the interruptions of windows, doors, cabinets, and ventilation hoods help to minimize any feeling of being closed in

by the tile. If you are using glass-fronted cabinets or open shelves, an extravagant but dramatic effect is to order cabinets without backs and tile behind them after hanging the cabinets. A tiled kitchen wall also provides an excellent opportunity to tile niches or shelves in matching or contrasting designs.

Where wall tile turns an outside corner in a busy part of a kitchen, say near the back door, edges may be vulnerable to chipping. The usual solutions would include installing bullnose trim pieces to turn the corner, using tiles with glazed edges, or mitering the edges of two rows of tile. In lieu of these, you may opt for a plastic edging strip. These long thin pieces are positioned under the last row of tile on each side and secured with adhesive. Such strips are available at any tile supplier in a wide array of colors and blend quite effectively with most ceramic surfaces.

## RANGE HOODS

In traditional Mexican and southern European kitchens, the range hood is often covered with tile. In addition to serving a practical purpose in terms of fire protection, a tiled hood can become the focal point of the room. Tile the whole hood in an elaborate treatment or simply run a border of tile below a stucco,

wood-faced, or metal hood. Either way, the tile on the hood surface should relate to that used on the surrounding areas. Since this area is subject to airborne grease, a glazed tile without a relief or textured design will be easier to keep clean. Most manufacturers make range hoods that can accommodate tile; or you can have one custom-made to fit a particular space or in a special shape. If your kitchen has a country European theme, a range hood of an appropriate shape and tile treatment will add appreciably to the look of authenticity. Often the range hood is tiled on the diagonal to contrast with the tile design elsewhere in the room. If you are tiling the wall behind the range and the hood, vary the placement or color for interest. An indoor grill can be treated in a similar fashion.

## OTHER USES

Ceramic tile can be used almost everywhere in the kitchen, including the proverbial kitchen sink. A tiled sink of any size and depth can be constructed on site to match your tile counters. As with counters, the primary maintenance issue is not the tile, but the grout. Your installer will probably use epoxy grout or another grout formulated for stain resistance. You may prefer to reserve this idea for an auxiliary bar or prep sink that gets less use.

As an alternative to taking tile all the way up the wall, consider tiling the backsplash and then repeating the treatment on the soffit above the upper cabinets, which is usually dead space. Or vary the soffit treatment for emphasis. A tile mural depicting life-size majolica plates, pitchers, and jars that appear to sit on a shelf would be a playful addition to the area. A more limited use of tile is to run a border of tiles at the base of the soffit and again at the ceiling line.

**ABOVE:** Hand-painted Portuguese tile murals adorn a cooktop's backsplash, while color-linked field tile, decorative trims, and molding enhance the soaring, wall-mounted hood. **OPPOSITE:** A ceiling-mounted copper and wood range hood over a cooktop is trimmed on four sides with a single row of Talisman's vine-motif relief tiles.

Tile wainscots work beautifully on kitchen walls without cabinets, and they can also define a breakfast area. Line up the top of the wainscot with the windowsill, the bottom of the upper cabinets, or another existing line to avoid a choppy look. Or use a single row of tile molding as a chair rail to define an eating area or relate to a border used elsewhere in the room. The back side of a work island, a peninsula, and the front of an eating bar are also logical and highly visible places to use tile. Repeat the same design used on a backsplash or range hood or vary it slightly.

## Input on Outlets

Why spoil a beautiful tile installation with poorly placed electrical outlets? Local electrical codes require the installation of outlets at frequent intervals, which can intrude upon a tile surface. To ensure that it is the tiles, and not the outlets, that get noticed, plan the placement of electrical outlets carefully *before* the tiles are installed. There are two options you should discuss with your electrician or contractor. One is an electrical strip that contains outlets at frequent intervals. It can be hidden directly beneath the upper cabinets and above the tile. The disadvantage to this option is that the appliance cords can distract from the beauty of your backsplash. If you don't want to unplug appliances after every use, the other choice is to place the outlets 6 to 8 inches above the counter; again, local code may specify their height.

Plan exactly where each will go and take that into consideration when designing the backsplash. Ask the electrician to leave the electrical box loose before you install the tile, which allows play of about 6 inches to the left or right direction so that you are not forced to place an outlet where it interferes with the design. You can buy ceramic switch plates or faux paint metal ones to match; some tile artists will provide switch plates to match hand-painted designs.

**OPPOSITE:** Liberally applied to backsplash, counters, even the base of the center island, Mexican tile displays its colorful exuberance in this kitchen designed by Anne James. **TOP LEFT:** The undermount salad sink is trimmed with cut pieces of quarter-round molding, known as horse teeth. **TOP RIGHT:** In lieu of an outside corner piece, the installer used narrow pieces of quarter-round. **ABOVE:** More horse teeth form the curved profile of the backsplash beside the range.

# 5

# In the Bath

*Our first stop in the morning, a frequent destination throughout the day, and the last thing we see before we hop into bed, the bathroom may be the smallest room in the house, but it looms large in importance. In recent years Americans have awakened to what Europeans have long known, that the bath should be as welcoming and nurturing as any of our more social spaces.*

*Bathrooms must fulfill a host of expectations: We demand that they be functional, hygienic, and safe, but we also expect them to serve as a place of ritual. A long soak in a bubble bath represents a retreat from the world of work and family responsibilities. Often the sole hideaway in the house, a bathroom must be attractive and serene, ideally zoning the private areas of toilet and bidet from the often shared spaces of sink, tub, and shower.*

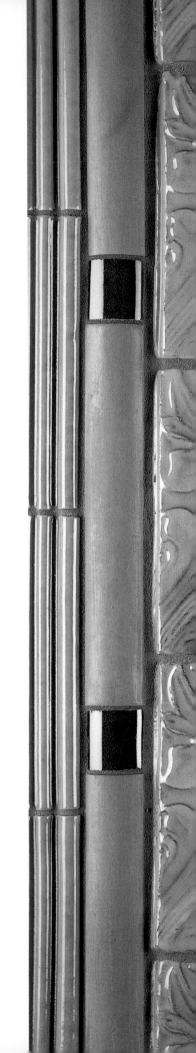

Ceramic tile can play a strong role in establishing the function and beauty of a bathroom, all the while concealing the room's flaws and highlighting its strengths.

## PRACTICALITIES

If cleanliness is next to godliness, God would be happy in a tile bathroom. Ceramic tile is an ideal material for a room with an inherently humid environment and the need for hygienic surfaces. Mold, mildew, and bacteria cannot permeate most tile surfaces and can be removed easily with a regular wipe-down, along with any buildup of soap scum. Still, exposure to water is insidious, requiring exacting installation procedures (see Water Protection, page 175). High temperatures from hot water and steam showers put further demands on bathroom installations.

Although vast improvements have been made in grout technology in the last decade, it is especially important that bathroom grout be well maintained so there is no opportunity for water to get behind the tile. One way to minimize problems with grout is to use larger tiles in areas that remain wet a good deal of the time; relatively fewer joints mean less reliance on grout. Cove trim tiles also help eliminate vulnerable grout lines between floor and wall and at corners. Likewise, bullnose tiles that handle 90-degree-angle transitions mean grout is not exposed to undue wear at corners.

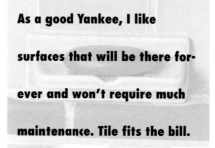

As a good Yankee, I like surfaces that will be there forever and won't require much maintenance. Tile fits the bill.

—Ann E. Grasso, Spatial Designer

Unlike a kitchen, a bathroom is not particularly subject to scratches and stains, meaning that just about any tile is appropriate for walls. But for shower, tub, and sauna floors, it is essential that you select a slip-resistant tile. Matte-glazed tiles or those with a subtle texture are the best choices. Highly glazed tiles can be dangerously slippery, while those with a gritty surface may be difficult to keep clean. Tiles used on the bathroom floor and in a shower enclosure should also have a low water absorption rate.

## DESIGN CONSIDERATIONS

Tempting as it is to buy a lovely tile, then make it work come hell or high water, the bathroom is not the place to yield to such temptation. It is almost always preferable to start by working out the placement of fixtures, windows and doors, and storage. Next give thought to the room's inherent features. Does it open directly onto a bedroom with a distinct color scheme? Consider how you can enhance the bathroom's assets and compensate for its drawbacks. Is it spacious or cramped, naturally light-filled or cave-like? Think about the mood you want to establish: Do you want to feel soothed or invigorated in the space? Then and only then should the matters of which tile and where to use it arise. For example, if your bathroom is blessed with a large window framing a lovely view, you may well want to select a quiet color or textured surface instead of a bold tile that competes with nature's own design. Likewise, numerous openings for doors, windows, shelves, and the like will interrupt any sort of mural treatment or an allover pattern. You may choose to use one tile for both floor and walls to "erase" odd jogs and create a cocoon of serenity. On the other hand, in a bathroom without much intrinsic architectural interest, a dramatic treatment involving three or four related tile designs could relieve visual boredom. Or a mixture of primary colors could brighten a room lacking in natural light.

More than any other space, a bathroom offers the opportunity to make ceramic tile the dominant design element. Furniture placement and fabric choices are not primary concerns; nor is there the plethora of functions that must be served by materials, as there is in the kitchen. Still, tile must be considered in relation to the other decorative elements in the room. If you want to match tile color to sinks, tubs, and other plumbing fixtures, look into programs established by several tile companies with leading plumbing manufacturers. (See American Olean, Dal-Tile, Florida Tile, and Summitville in the Directory of Resources, pages 191 to 192.)

These prematched designs assist the homeowner who wants to play it safe. However, more personal looks can be achieved by freely mixing tiles and fixtures. By tile selection alone, you can pay homage to a vintage Victorian, complement an Arts and Crafts look, or create an inviting space for young children. If you opt for different tile treatments on the floor and wall, you may want to come up with a linking device such as repeating the wall tile as an inset or border on the floor. Likewise, a vanity counter

**PRECEDING PAGES, LEFT:** Glazed tiles randomly arranged fill a shower stall fitted with a teak grille. **CENTER:** Molded woodland motifs are in the Arts and Crafts tradition. **RIGHT:** A leaf border is trimmed with a terra-cotta liner antiqued with aquamarine grout. **THIS PAGE:** A sophisticated mix of glazed tile, tumbled marble, and ceramic mosaics is used slightly differently on each of the four walls in this bathroom. On the tub's long wall, marble dominates, with ceramic reserved for trim. A harlequin pattern gives both materials equal play on either side of the vanity. On another wall, tile clads the wainscot, with marble as an accent.

**OPPOSITE:** In this Miami-area bath inspired by Moorish architecture, mosaic artist Luciano trimmed veined marble on the floor and steps with tiny squares of glass. On the floor's perimeter, mosaics are arranged randomly; the baseboard is treated to a geometric pattern. **ABOVE:** In an equally fantastical bathroom in Santa Fe, custom-made tiles by Counterpoint set into plaster shape a banana tree, turtle, and parrot, evoking a tropical island.

## Ceramic Accessories

Placement and style of soap dishes, toothbrush and glass holders, toilet paper holders, towel bars, and hooks should all be determined *before* your tile is installed. Attention to such seemingly small details is what distinguishes a well-planned tile installation. There are two schools of thought when it comes to accessories. They can be regarded as bathroom jewelry, to be shown off, or as elements that distract from the beauty of tile, to be hidden or played down. Tile and plumbing suppliers stock generic ceramic accessories in white, beige, and the common pastels in both glossy and matte finishes. Depending upon your tile selection, these may or may not coordinate well. Some manufacturers also produce

accessory pieces that match specific lines of their tile—at significantly higher prices; some companies will custom-make accessories to match any tile.

Ceramic accessory pieces are bonded to the substrate and grouted in place alongside the tile. Some protrude from the surface; others are inset flush with the tile and require preparation of the wall before installation. Towel bars may be set within the field tile or above it, depending upon how high the wall is tiled. Soap dishes and other accessories made of chrome, brass, and tempered glass mount on the tile itself or above it. Towel bars and their brackets are often made of metal and are mounted directly on the tile.

Another option is to eliminate the need for accessories whenever possible. You can avoid protruding soap dishes that interrupt the tile pattern by creating tiled ledges or recesses around sinks, tubs, or showers. With a large tub deck, you may prefer to keep soaps and sponges in a basket or a low wooden or ceramic bowl. And hooks are less conspicuous than towel bars.

**OPPOSITE:** Architect Dana Cantelmo revitalized a dark New York City bath by playfully tiling every conceivable surface, revealing the design flexibility inherent in solid-color tile. Two checkered patterns form a wainscot; wooden doors are inset flush with the tiled vanity. **ABOVE LEFT:** A coordinated soap dish blends into the color scheme. **TOP RIGHT:** Ceramic towel hooks are less obtrusive than bars. **ABOVE RIGHT:** Borders and cove molding acknowledge the transition to the ceiling, which is also tiled.

might echo the floor's design motif. Some of the most interesting bathrooms deftly mix two or more materials. Marble, granite, limestone, slate, and glass tile can work beautifully in combination with ceramic tile, as can redwood, cedar, pecky cypress, and other moisture-hardy woods. (Avoid using wood in wet areas, where it may absorb water, expand, and crack adjacent tile.) Solid surfacing can be milled and routed to form a frame for tile or can accommodate flush insets.

Tiled areas can improve the architecture of a bathroom. If space allows, consider installing a tile bench, perhaps with storage below, making a convenient perch for removing socks and shoes or holding extra towels. A terry-cloth cushion would be a nice added touch. Framing out one wall over the tub or using the space between studs to create a tiled niche offers other storage opportunities, whether fitted with shelves that are themselves tiled or made of glass. For privacy in a shared bath, you can frame out a half or full wall beside the toilet, then tile it on both sides.

## A LOT OR A LITTLE?

Tiling an entire bathroom, as is the norm in Italy, unifies the space. All four walls are typically sheathed to the ceiling in one or more colors or designs. The floor is always tiled and often the ceiling is as well. When the tile is beautiful, the effect can be stunning and luxurious. A border may acknowledge the transition from a smaller tile to a larger one, or a trim treatment accentuate the shape of a window. The full-dress treatment eliminates awkward junctures where tile meets paint, wallpaper, or wood moldings. However, in a small room, wall-to-wall tile can be confining, and even larger baths that use only one tile design can seem monotonous. With a total tile treatment it is often important to soften the effect with accessories—fluffy towels, fabric at the windows, plants, and the like.

The classic American approach has been to tile the tub area to the ceiling or close to it, then use a tile wainscot elsewhere. But there is no hard-and-fast rule. Some designers like to tile all the walls, others prefer to tile one or two and use another finish on the remaining walls. Some tile only the tub/shower area and the backsplash above a vanity. Others feel it is essential to tile the splash area behind the toilet and bidet for sanitary reasons. A full- or

**RIGHT:** A mix of reproduction William De Morgan and William Morris tiles form a striking tub surround that reaches to the ceiling.

## Types of Tubs

The standard bathtub is designed to sit against a wall, exposing its front panel, or apron. Except for old or reproduction freestanding tubs, which rest on feet or a base, all tubs are designed in two parts, allowing you to omit the apron and cover the area with tile or another material instead. Whether made of porcelain-enameled steel or cast iron, acrylic, or fiberglass, most modern tubs can also be ordered with one or more sides unfinished for custom installations. For a completely built-in treatment, drop-in models are also available.

When tiling around a tub, it is essential that access to the workings of the tub be provided in case of a blockage or leak. Your tile installer can devise a removable tiled panel that blends into the surrounding tile. Likewise, whirlpool tubs require access to the electric pump, which can be hidden behind a tiled panel located in the apron area or nearby.

three-quarter-height treatment is preferable to tiling only halfway up the wall, which creates an awkward tension between two similar-size areas.

A well-chosen tile can make a small bath seem larger; another could make a large space seem cozier. One design used in quantity can produce a wonderfully serene environment; another used in the same space could convey luxury. A small amount of superb tile can create great drama—for example, a mural in a shower, surrounded by simple white squares. A delicately hand-painted tile could be used in a tub surround, then reappear as a chair rail on the other walls dividing two colors of paint. On a tub wall with a nondescript window, the tile could frame the opening on the sides and top it off with a dramatic ziggurat. Beyond covering areas subject to water, each use is a response to the shape of the room and the tile itself. Treatments need not be identical on all walls or parts of the room. The same two or three tiles, used in varying arrangements, could effectively zone different areas and functions, yet retain a harmonious look.

## AROUND THE TUB

The tub surround—the three walls above and around a tub that is installed against a wall—is the most commonly tiled area and often the one that allows the greatest creative license, thanks to its large expanse. Here is the place for a special treatment, whether a mural, a pattern created from two or more tiles, a series of tiled panels inset into field tile, or mir-rors on one or more sides bordered in tiles. When a tub is used only for taking baths—thanks to a freestanding shower—it may not be necessary to tile the whole wall. Likewise, a whirlpool tub placed in a wide deck or against a window does not require a full tile treatment on surrounding walls. A single or double course of tiles immediately

**OPPOSITE:** Elaborate borders by Native Tile distinguish a tub surround and apron and frame a tiled niche. A row of trim smoothes the transition to the drop-in tub. **ABOVE LEFT:** Another built-in tub gets a tiled deck of hand-molded Mexican tile. Multicolor tile accents the curved windows. **TOP RIGHT:** In lieu of a front tub panel, tile provides a unified look. **ABOVE RIGHT:** Three tile colors add visual excitement on the surround behind a standard tub.

**ABOVE:** A shower's stone bench and intricate tile work provide safety and beauty. The floor is unglazed terra-cotta tile. **OPPOSITE, FROM TOP:** White tile laid in a running band links shower walls to the rest of the room. A tiled seat and niche echo curved lines used elsewhere in a family bath; the seat is sloped to keep standing water from damaging the grout. Shimmering glazed tile by Counterpoint minimizes the sense of enclosure in a shower stall.

above the tub or the tub deck may be all that is necessary. If children use the tub, play it safe and tile up the wall to protect against splashes. When a tub or whirlpool sits up against a window, a tile frame can draw attention to the view and a tile sill will alleviate water damage. Or, depending upon the proportion of the window to the wall, it may look better to tile the entire wall.

If the shower is in the tub itself, consider how you will protect the room from water. A clear glass shower door will reveal your tile design; a shower curtain will hide all or part of it, as will opaque or translucent glass doors.

By placing the tub a foot or two out from the wall, you can provide room for a tiled deck, an expansive touch that lends valuable space for shampoo bottles and other bathing needs. When the tub surround is tiled, covering the apron (the tub's front panel) and deck (the horizontal surface around the tub) in the same tile unifies the space and tends to make it look larger. When the apron and deck are tiled to match the floor, the look is equally clean-lined and dramatic.

## IN THE SHOWER

As with tubs, a separate shower surround offers a relatively large expanse for tile decoration. The shower can be the focal point of a tile installation, or an overall tile motif can continue into the shower area uninterrupted, depending upon the type of shower and door treatment. A shower may be built to custom specifications on site, with two or three solid walls covered with tile, stone, glass block, or solid surfacing. Or the

## Bench Strategy

For safety and comfort, particularly if children or older persons use a shower, consider including a tiled bench. The seat, which should be slightly sloped into the shower to channel the water into the drain, can be framed with two-by-fours, sheathed in exterior-grade plywood, and then topped with a waterproof membrane and cementitious backer board. Alternatively, a waterproof mud-bed installation can be employed. If possible, use curved trim pieces at corners and edges to minimize grout stress in vulnerable places.

**OPPOSITE:** Inspired by a painting of an interior by Impressionist artist Pierre Bonnard, mosaic artist Stephen Spretnjak used more than fifty colors of Venetian glass tile on all surfaces, layering an angled rug over a field of solid color. **THIS PAGE, TOP LEFT:** A small waterfall splashes against an abstract tile mosaic over the vanity. **TOP RIGHT:** Irregular color blocking is used in the shower stall. **ABOVE:** The rug "drapes" perfectly over the sill of the shower stall.

Elevated tubs that are reached by steps have become an unfortunate fad in bathroom design. Such installations can be extremely hazardous, even when a railing is used. The inherent risk of slipping on a wet surface, whether it is tile or another material, is simply not worth the dramatic effect. Tubs installed at floor level that require stepping down into them are equally hazardous in terms of entry and exit, and present a risk of someone (particularly a child or elderly person) inadvertently falling into the tub in a darkened bathroom.

walls that protrude into the room can be made of tempered glass with an integral glass door. (A shower stall can also be designed so that a door is unnecessary.) Standard "clear" glass takes on a green cast when it is of a certain thickness; you may want to specify low-iron glass, which has no greenish cast and will not distort the color of your tile. Some prefabricated showers, typically made of fiberglass or acrylic, come with all sides finished and preclude the use of tile. Others offer one or two sides of glass or plastic and can be installed against a tile wall.

Provision for secure footing is essential. Be sure to use slip-resistant tiles for the shower floor. Ceramic mosaics are often used because the large number of grout lines help form a slip-resistant surface. A shower floor may be set in mortar over a prefab metal or fiberglass pan (a shallow-sided base) with a special tiling lip. A tile setter may opt for a waterproof membrane under a mud-set installation instead. (See Water Protection, page 175.) Either way, it is essential that the floor slope gently to allow for proper drainage. Instead of a tile floor you may elect to use a prefabricated fiberglass shower pan, even if the rest of the room is tiled.

It's a good idea to tile the ceiling above a shower since the area will be subjected to vapor, which condenses into water. A steam shower will of necessity have to have a ceiling. In fact, you may choose to tile the entire bathroom ceiling for continuity. Ceiling tile is traditionally laid on the

diagonal so it doesn't "fight" with the grid of the wall tiles. Ceiling tile must be installed properly so that it does not fall off. Your installer should use a high-bond setting material to secure the tile.

## AROUND THE SINK

If the tub and shower experience the equivalent of mini-monsoons, the bathroom sink is exposed to spring rain, a regular if less violent occurrence, making a waterproof backsplash and counter a necessity. Tile treatment depends upon sink selection; types divide roughly into the freestanding variety and those that are installed in a vanity. The former may be wall-mounted or pedestal style; a few rest on metal or porcelain legs. Freestanding styles sometimes have an integral shallow backsplash, as do some vanity counters, although this doesn't preclude installing a deeper tile backsplash above. A wall-mounted or pedestal sink also reveals a good section of the wall below, offering another chance to show off tile.

Handsome and sculptural, pedestal and wall-mounted sinks also create the illusion of more space in a room. However, they offer no storage beneath and minimal surface above for toiletries, and their plumbing connections are exposed. Tile can be used to solve these problems, while maintaining the clean look such styles offer. Rather than sit directly against the wall, both pedestal and wall-mounted sinks can be placed against a framed-out box that sits out from the wall 6 to 8 inches and can extend to the floor or stop short of it. The box will hide the plumbing (provision for access in case of a leak is essential) and can be tiled on the top and sides, providing some surface area without the bulk of a vanity. Alternatively, a shallow tiled ledge or a recess set between the studs above the sink deck can provide storage, although neither will hide plumbing. Taller recesses placed on either side of a pedestal—or between a pair of them—can take the place of a medicine chest.

While a vanity provides ample storage, it obscures all or part of the wall. (An alternative is to "hang" a vanity on the wall, rather than have it sit on the floor, a boon in smaller rooms—the uninterrupted floor area gives a feeling of greater space.) A sink in a vanity will need a backsplash, but there is no need to tile behind the unit itself. However, be sure to work out the wall tile design to acknowledge the interruption gracefully. Another

option is to frame out a box, creating spaces for doors and drawers, and then tile the surfaces; this affords the convenience of a vanity without a distracting change in material.

Tile is an ideal surface for a vanity top, although you need to tailor your installation to your sink type. Countertop sinks come in several styles: self-rimming, in which the sink lip overlaps the countertop surface; flush, installed with a metal ring that bridges the two materials; integral, actually molded as part of a solid-surfacing or cultured marble countertop; or undermounted, in which the counter sits above the sink. Self-rimming sinks work well with tile counters, but standard flush mounts are difficult to keep clean, and the metal band is not particularly appealing. Preferable is a ceramic sink especially designed to be grouted flush to coordinated tile. Undermount sinks are designed for a slab of marble or solid surfacing, although they too can be used with tile if the transition between sink and

**OPPOSITE, LEFT:** A classic pedestal sink shows off a decorative wall treatment. The diagonally laid baseboard and a relief border handle the transition to the floor; reproductions of Julia Morgan's Deer Creek relief border tiles define the top of the wainscot.
**OPPOSITE, RIGHT:** A drop-in sink gracefully overlaps a ceramic mosaic vanity top.
**ABOVE:** An undermount sink is neatly installed with cut pieces of bullnose tile.

counter is handled with small curved trim tiles. Some artisans make small hand-thrown ceramic sinks that can be paired with matching tile, a nice touch for a powder room or guest bath. A one-of-a-kind sink can also be crafted on site from small or broken tiles to match or contrast with a tile counter.

In general, a bathroom vanity surface is similar to a kitchen counter. When tiling around a sink, arrange the design from the sink edge outward, so that there are as few cuts as possible and that they are placed inconspicuously. Usually a design starts at the center of the surface so the two sides are balanced. You may want to adjust the pattern slightly to minimize cuts. But be careful that this doesn't throw off other components, such as a pair of mirrors hung over the vanity. If you are considering a deliberately asymmetrical layout, work it out completely before setting a single tile. As in kitchens, take care to work out the placement of electrical outlets in advance, so they can be convenient and adhere to local codes without intruding on your tile design. (One advantage of a vanity is that outlets can be installed inside the box or on its sides rather than on the tiled wall.)

## WALL TREATMENTS

Visits to tile showrooms are particularly helpful when it comes to figuring out how to deal with the inherent challenges of a small space broken up by fixtures, vanities, doors, and windows. You'll also get ideas for details that can make any bathroom more appealing. For example, consider using:

- Small murals or inset designs made up of four or six tiles over the toilet or between two windows.
- A mural—perhaps of a garden view—to create the illusion of more space in a bathroom with no window.
- A tile medallion between a pair of sinks with separate mirrors.
- Two or three borders set low on the wall to define the transition between wall and floor.

Pay particular attention to border treatments. Remember that borders attract the eye, so there should be a logic to their placement, whether above a baseboard, at towel-bar height, or where a wall meets the ceiling. Recessed medicine chests can be bordered with one or more courses of tile. A mirror can be treated to a tile frame for a finished look.

## Children's Bathrooms

When designing a children's bathroom, remember how quickly they grow up. Resist the impulse to install tiles with precious motifs like ducks or bunnies. Such designs will be outgrown quickly and they could affect the resale value of your house. Instead, consider:

- White mixed with a bold or pastel color.
- A playful multicolor combination.
- Natural elements such as fish or leaves.
- Geometric symbols or other abstract designs that will "grow" with the child.
- A solid-color tile and youthful accents in wallcovering, shower curtain, and other easily substituted accessories.
- If you cannot resist a juvenile component, limit it to a tile border that can be replaced at a future date.

**OPPOSITE:** In a bathroom shared by four siblings, Blue Slide Art Tile's designs add a whimsical touch that is not overly "cute." A border of frogs, turtles, and other critters topped with a rainbow of solid-color tiles sets the playful mood. Above relief molding, colorful "dots" notch into some corners of white field tile. A second checkerboard border reprises the one below and lowers the apparent height of the room. **ABOVE:** Designer Deborah Lipner indulged a youngster's love of Dumbo and his cohorts with an Elephant Walk border separating tile colors and layouts; both it and the wall field tile are also by Blue Slide.

Borders around mirrors or sections of tile should be symmetrical from top to bottom and side to side. Work these elements out before any tile is cut or laid. Also consider:

- Will the pattern be centered?
- Will the corners be mitered or will the pieces simply meet?
- If the corners are mitered, how can you avoid spoiling the flow of the design?
- Is incorporating a coordinated or contrasting small square tile at each corner a better solution than a mitered or overlapped treatment?
- If the tile must be cut to fit, where is the best place to hide the cuts?

When contemplating a tile frame treatment, remember that a flush-mounted mirror will literally "mirror" each tile. In the case of a border, the impact is enhanced by being doubled, but when field tile butts against a mirror, a pattern such as a checkerboard can be seriously compromised. The solution is a run of half tiles that meets the mirror, which will read as full tiles and still allow the pattern to come out right in the corners of the room.

Mirrors can enhance or compete with tile designs. For example, a mural on the wall directly opposite a mirror can be enjoyed every time you brush your hair or check your makeup. But a pattern on an angled wall or that turns a corner may create confusing repetitions in the reflected images of tile.

## COLOR CONSIDERATIONS

Before deciding on a tile color scheme, think about several other aspects of bath design. The two most dominant materials in any bath are tile and fixtures. Using one color or closely related colors will unify the space; bold color contrasts will enliven it. But bright-colored fixtures that contrast with field tiles will draw attention to the fixtures rather than integrate them into the whole scheme. This may be desirable in a bathroom with sculptural pedestal sinks, but might be jarring in a more traditional scheme.

Color also affects the illusion of space, with pale colors

making a room look larger and dark ones making it seem cozier and smaller. Pale neutrals and pastels, particularly in warmer tones, tend to flatter the skin. Green, blue, and cooler colors may make skin look sallow, although warm fluorescent lighting can offset this effect. Good lighting is crucial for safety, as well as for grooming and applying makeup. Dark colors may be dramatic, but plan additional lighting to compensate. Glazed tiles will reflect more light than matte. Maintenance is another factor in selecting colored bathroom tile. Dirt cannot hide in a white room, and dark colors show soap scum more readily than lighter ones.

Finally, think about color in relation to materials elsewhere in the house. Do you want the bathroom and adjoining bedroom to have a related palette? Remember that it is far easier to replace curtains and a bedspread than tiled walls and fixtures. A classic color scheme may be your choice for a master bath, while a bolder, more colorful approach may be just the ticket in a less used guest bathroom.

**OPPOSITE:** A border designed by Gail Green in tumbled marble mosaic accents white Italian tile. Thanks to precise placement, the pattern continues in the mirror image. **ABOVE:** Corners of a terra-cotta relief border framing a mirror are carefully mitered so as not to interrupt the design. **BELOW:** The border design over a tub continues into a glass-shelved niche. Two-inch-square checkered tiles made of two shades of sea shells sit inside 4-inch-square Italian tiles designed to accommodate such smaller tiles. The border tiles align neatly with the 8-inch field tiles.

## FLOOR SHOW

Bathroom floors present special design challenges. Their small size and multitude of fixtures often result in a minimal unbroken area. This means that a bold or complex design may overpower the space and a border might exaggerate irregular shapes. In small or awkwardly shaped baths, consider a simple field tile, possibly laid on the diagonal. Or craft an overall pattern in 1- or 2-inch mosaics, perhaps in closely related colors.

While a bathroom may measure 7 feet by 10 feet from wall to wall, the floor space is actually much smaller, since tub, vanity, and commode intrude. Be sure to consider the width of the corridor formed by fixtures when selecting tile. If you have a 3-foot path from door to tub, for example, don't use a

**OPPOSITE, ABOVE AND BELOW:** Michelle Griffoul's freeform tile leaves set in cement offer slip-resistant footing in a shower for two. A tiled ledge is another safety feature, allowing users to wash their feet or shave their legs when seated. **ABOVE:** A cowboy and the cow that jumped over the moon meet up in Shel Neymark's hand-painted mural.

**RIGHT:** Miami designer Dennis Jenkins and tile retailer Sunny McLean created a tile montage behind their own bathtub. French glazed ogees angle off Mexican *saltillos,* reversed for greater texture, and squares of Mexican stone. **ABOVE:** Gold leaf walls reflect light off the tiled floor and an irregular wainscot in the toilet stall.

16-inch square tile which will require cuts that spoil its design; a 6-inch tile will work much better. Another option is to use a 12-inch tile laid on the diagonal. Borders can sometimes solve problems of scale. For instance, in a larger space, the 16-inch tiles could be banded with a 4-inch border to avoid most cuts.

Where a bathroom floor meets another floor of a different material and sometimes a slightly different height, a marble door saddle, or threshold, is typically used to bridge the transition. With a white or pale floor, the standard gray-veined white marble is suitable. But if you are using a dark or unusual color tile, you may want to use a darker color saddle. Discuss this with your designer or installer before ordering the tile.

# 6

# Around the House

There's no need to limit your use of tile to the expected areas, such as baths and kitchens. Once you've gotten your feet wet, why not jump in all the way? Entryways, sun porches, wet bars, laundry rooms, even living rooms and family rooms are equally deserving of attention. Whether as a fireplace surround, a wainscot, or accents like baseboards, stair risers, cove molding, and window borders, tile is perfectly at home throughout the house. And don't feel that innovative uses must be confined to architecture; tables, benches, mirrors, and other pieces of furniture respond well to ceramic adornment, and even urns and other rounded surfaces can receive pique assiette or ceramic mosaic treatments. Using tile in these purely decorative ways permits a freedom unknown in bathrooms or kitchens, where function makes clear demands.

Often a small, idiosyncratic project such as a corner ziggurat that steps down to the floor can bring as much visual pleasure as an extensive—and expensive—installation. And don't overlook the impact of displaying a single tile or a small mural as art, whether framed, set into plaster or stucco, or simply hung on the wall. Antique tiles salvaged from razed buildings and other one-of-a kind tiles are superb candidates for such treatment.

## WALL ART

Many cultures regard tiled walls as the norm in homes of the well-to-do. Precedent goes back thousands of years to the Middle East, where walls of mosques and palaces were traditionally covered with tiles. In Moorish Spain, intricately fitted mosaic tiles were more commonly used on walls than floors. In

> **Today there is a new golden age of tile.**
>
> —Norman Karlson, Country Floors

northern Europe, tiles originally were considered flooring material, but the pragmatic Dutch saw advantage in using them on walls as well. Built very close to the water and sometimes actually below sea level, the lowlanders' houses were extremely damp, causing whitewash on the walls to flake off. To inhibit water from wicking up the walls from the damp floors, the Dutch began using tile for baseboards. With the passage of time, the use of tile extended up the walls, where it also provided better insulation and fireproofing than wood paneling.

The mania for tiled walls soon spread to Germany and Russia. The eighteenth-century palaces of the Pagodenburg near Munich and the Menshikov Palace in St. Petersburg were extravagant in their use of decorative Dutch tiles on walls and even ceilings. Some of the most elaborate walls appeared in Portugal, which originally imported Dutch tiles and then began producing its own increasingly flamboyant designs. Whole rooms were "wallpapered" with tile, as were the facades of churches, monasteries, and public buildings. In the New World, colonial Mexico imitated Spanish tastes and splashed their walls with domestically made tiles. By the nineteenth century, a galloping English tile industry produced enough inexpensive tiles for a growing middle class to fill their homes. Molded, transferware, and silk-screen tiles, often in murals, dominated many a Victorian foyer, dining room, and parlor; even nurseries were paneled with tiles with subjects ranging from favorite children's books to morally uplifting themes.

## FUNCTION MEETS BEAUTY

Tile makes a memorable first impression, serving as the perfect introduction to a house. On a practical level, its resistance to dampness makes it ideal for an entrance hall, which is exposed to changes in temperature and humidity. The backdoor equivalent of a foyer, a mudroom is equally deserving of tile work. If you install tile on the walls and floors, regular wipe-downs will keep the area looking crisp and new. And nothing provides a better backdrop below a coatrack than a tile wainscot, which can stand up to hard knocks from sports equipment and backpacks. A laundry room is another ideal venue for water- and stain-resistant tile.

In a sunroom, tiling the walls beneath the windows can extend the outdoor feeling. In any south-facing room, tile-clad floors and walls can also act as passive solar collectors, absorbing and storing heat, then releasing it in the cool of the evening. Darker colored, unglazed, or matte-glazed tiles ½ inch thick or more perform most effectively.

## Mosaic Murals

Some murals are more properly ceramic mosaics in that differently colored pieces of ceramic tile form an abstract or figurative design, similar to the process used with glass or stone. (*Ceramic mosaic* is also an industry term used to denote small tiles.) *Pique assiette,* the French term literally meaning "broken plate," also known as "rubble," is one form of tile mosaic in which irregular pieces of cut or broken tile are laid out in designs, then grouted in place. This flamboyant technique is a wonderful way to use up extra pieces of tile, factory seconds, or odd lots. Another type of mosaic involves individual component tiles that are actually shaped to fit together, like pieces of a jigsaw puzzle.

**PRECEDING PAGES, LEFT:** Tiles cut into triangles applied to stair risers point the way up and down. **CENTER:** A terra-cotta and ceramic mosaic baseboard relates to the pattern on the floor. **RIGHT:** These trim pieces are imported from Italy. **THIS PAGE:** A wainscot of hand-painted Mexican tile offers a splash-proof surface behind an impromptu bar. Solid-color squares laid diagonally are framed by decorative borders.

Baseboards are another ideal locale for tile, in lieu of vulnerable painted wood. Since you need use only one tier of tile, a baseboard is also an opportunity to use more expensive tile than elsewhere. Here tile can be treated playfully, blue and yellow squares interspersed, for example, or three or four colors randomly mixed. Choose cove-base tiles with a bullnose edge or top standard tile with a curved trim piece that allows a smooth transition to the flat plane of the wall without trapping dust. If tile is used elsewhere in the room, perhaps on a fireplace surround or a window border, you may want to repeat it on the baseboard. For a more restrained approach, you can simply extend the floor tile to the baseboard, using appropriate trim pieces. Tile baseboards work equally well with wood floors.

Tiled stair risers, baseboards' upwardly mobile cousins, are another showcase for tile's inherent drama, and extremely practical to boot. Unlike wood risers, which have to be painted more frequently than other trim, tile will not show scuffs or become dented. For safety's sake, however, it is crucial that tile be perfectly applied to the riser surface in order to avoid gaps or irregularities that could cause someone to trip. For neatness, you may want to trim the outside edges of the risers with narrow wood molding. Once you have worked out these essentials, give your imagination free rein. Tile risers can continue a motif established on the first floor—in baseboards, for example—or stand on their own. Have some fun with these possibilities:

- Create a checkerboard effect, perhaps with ceramic mosaics.
- Use a different color tile on each riser, shading from green to blue, for example, or across the full spectrum.
- Use a different but related design, such as handcrafted Mexican Talavera squares, on each tier.
- Use vertical stripes to increase the illusion of height or horizontal ones to make a narrow stair seem wider.

## WAINSCOTS AND CHAIR RAILS

Traditionally made of paneled wood or beaded board, but equally handsome and more durable in tile, wainscotting extends up the wall 3 or 4 feet to protect the surfaces most exposed to dirt and dings. In the Craftsman era, wainscots reached even higher, sometimes lining up with the tops of windows for a strong horizontal line. There are no rigid rules about height, although in a small

**OPPOSITE:** A wainscot of Spanish squares linked with star corner medallions is topped with a border of hand-painted celestial symbols. **ABOVE:** Tiles left over from larger projects and banded in wood liven up a windowless laundry room.

room with few windows a high wainscot may induce claustrophobia. In a dining room a wainscot usually reaches 32 to 36 inches, or chair rail height, to protect painted or wallpapered surfaces above from damage by chairs pushed back from the table. In a family breakfast area, wainscotted walls are a marvelous defense against sticky fingers and splashed apple juice.

Because dining rooms traditionally do not have carpets or upholstered furniture, they allow enormous leeway for tile to be the dominant element on both floor and walls. If you plan to top a tile wainscot with wallpaper, pick the permanent material first, then the paper. You may opt for a subtle relief tile rather than a bold pattern, which will allow you greater options in a wallpaper. When the wainscot is the star of the room, the decorative possibilities are endless. You can:

- Enliven an existing wood wainscot with a row of ornately decorated or relief tiles installed above it.
- Top a solid-color tile with a decorative border.
- Run tile on the diagonal to make the space look larger.
- Finish the top of a diagonal placement with angled pieces for an informal look.
- Use curved or otherwise shaped tiles for the top row.
- Use tile moldings or border pieces with field tile to create the effect of panels.

**ABOVE:** In the Netherlands, tile wainscoting is a practical solution for the low-lying damp terrain. These seventeenth-century Royal Makkum tiles are original to the house.
**RIGHT:** A high wainscot tiled to suggest a patchwork quilt handles damp clothes and muddy boots in the back hall of a Dutch house.

- Use variations of the basic design on one or more sides of the room.
- If space allows, continue a wainscot into a narrow display shelf or buffet shelf.
- Repeat a motif used as a baseboard atop the wainscot.
- Mix tile with wood moldings or strips.
- Fill in panels of a wood wainscot with tile insets.

If a full wainscot would overpower a space or require too much work or investment in tile, try a tile chair rail instead. Used in this fashion, one or more trim pieces can have a powerful impact on a room. Or be more assertive and extend the chair rail design up and around the windows and doors. For a less permanent installation, "float" a row of tile between two strips of wood molding. (The tile can be mounted on plywood and removed when you move.) Or apply a row of squares laid point to point.

Wainscots are not just for dining areas and halls. In a bedroom, use a tile wainscot at a 3-foot height, then go up the wall another couple of feet to define one or two headboards. In a child's bedroom, a chair rail frieze of brightly colored triangles or a free-form design of butterflies or pine trees could add a charming touch.

# Ideas to Burn

A fireplace's role as the focal point of a room suggests the use of unusual or dramatic tiles, and its relatively small area encourages embellishment with borders and trim pieces. Rather than replace an old mantel, you can dress it with tile held in place by molding, or simply tile right over it. (You may need to box it out with plywood first.) Likewise, an existing surround can be tiled over. In any case, plan tile placement to minimize tile cuts. Here are some suggested fireplace treatments:

• Install a decorative tile frieze above the mantel or in lieu of a mantel.

• Decorate the chimney breast with a tile mural.
• Flank the opening with a series of tiles depicting painted or relief columns or pilasters, perhaps topped with tiles forming a lintel.
• Create a harlequin-effect surround with squares of several solid colors set diagonally.
• Emulate the Victorians with a pair of tile mural panels flanking the mantelpiece.
• Use a deep relief tile molding to form a mantel.
• Continue the floor tile onto the hearth and up the chimney breast for a unified look.
• Build shallow tile shelves on the chimney breast to display sculpture or ceramics.
• Revitalize a flat fireplace surround or an uninteresting mantelpiece with *pique assiette,* or broken tile.
• Spice up a "too serious" mantel with a surround of brightly colored tiles, in either a geometric or a random placement.
• Continue the glazed tile used on the surround into the fire chamber itself, so that the fireplace can stand on its own merits during the warmer months.
• With a traditional surround, leave room for a decorative panel, perhaps a mural, beneath the mantel.

**ABOVE:** A traditional English floor covering, encaustic tiles are made of several colors of damp clay; unlike a surface glaze, when fired the designs actually become part of the clay body. **RIGHT:** A kitchen fireplace is faced with a collage of reproductions of nineteenth-century English encaustic and a few relief tiles, all made by L'Esperance Tile Works.

# FIREPLACES

Tile's fireproof properties make it an especially suitable material for trimming a fireplace. Historically, unglazed tiles or bricks were used to reduce the risk of fire in wooden houses. Today, such materials continue to provide an all-important safety zone between the fire and the room itself. Formed in the intense heat of a kiln, tile is so fire-resistant that it was used to construct the decorative and highly efficient wood-burning stoves that have heated central and northern European homes from the fourteenth century on.

Depending upon its style and size, the fireplace may offer a narrow three-sided surround within a wooden mantelpiece or far more extensive surfaces that can be decorated. An interesting tile treatment can effectively disguise a featureless fireplace or a flush-mounted prefabricated unit. In traditional fireplaces, the surround is covered with masonry or tile. But tile also can be used on the hearth and on the fireback; or it can form the mantelshelf or full mantelpiece; and even climb up the chimney breast. (Before making any modifications other than adding a tile veneer to an existing fireplace, be sure to check local codes and ascertain whether you need a permit to ensure a safe installation.) Hearth tile should be laid so that it is flush with the floor of the firebox and with the surrounding floor. If the hearth is raised above the level of the floor, the entire surface can be tiled.

To pay homage to a beautiful carved wood mantel, you may want to use a relatively quiet tile for a surround. On the other hand, when there is only a simple mantel or none at all, tile can play the starring role in this domestic drama. On a stucco or plaster fireplace, such as those often found in Tudor-style or southwestern houses, decorative possibilities are enormous and as individual as each hearth. A curved opening may need only a perimeter of tile to define its shape. If space allows, you may also be able to build a tiled recess beside or beneath the fireplace for log storage. A tiled inglenook, or fireplace nook, often

**ABOVE:** A little says a lot in this tiny fireplace whose curved top is accented with simple triangular tiles; above the mantelpiece, decorative triangles reiterate the motif. **OPPOSITE, TOP LEFT:** Designer Douglas Bartoli covered a massive chimney breast with an ambitious argyle pattern made primarily of square and rectangular tiles in various sizes. Log storage and a television hide behind copper doors. **TOP RIGHT:** Surround, hearth, and even the firebox itself are covered with relief tile copied from Victorian examples in the Mark Twain House in Hartford, Connecticut. **BELOW LEFT:** Artist Veva Crozler painted a flock of fire-breathing Chinese dragons on bisqued factory-made tiles, then refired them to create a fireplace surround in a Tudor-style house. **BELOW RIGHT:** In a rustic log house in Colorado, golden-hued tile in a pebble texture on a fireplace surround offers smart contrast to the predominant wood tones.

**PRECEDING PAGES:** A waterfall of glazed tile by L'Esperance, Pratt & Larsen, and Moravian Pottery & Tile Works mixed with tumbled marble dominates the sweeping staircase in this rustic Colorado lodge designed by Holly Leuders. On the chimney breast, glazed and bisqued Florentine mosaics by Moravian Pottery & Tile Works depict flowers and griffons, lions, and other animals. Alphabet tiles inset in the tiled fireplace surround spell out the name of the house. **ABOVE:** Original Malibu tiles cover the floor and stairs of the Adamson House—now a museum; the curvaceous baseboards were made specially for the house and are based on Moorish or Saracen designs. The steps are made of terra cotta; the landing floor is laid in a herringbone pattern. **OPPOSITE, ABOVE:** Antique tile murals were framed and hung rather than installed permanently in the wall. **OPPOSITE, BELOW:** A set of antique Mexican decorated terra-cotta tiles are displayed like works of art on the wall under a covered porch.

with built-in seating, represents the ultimate in coziness.

Most tiles can be used around the
firebox opening. The hearth will not be
walked on, but the tile should be strong
enough to withstand the shock of having
a heavy log dropped on it. Unglazed
quarry tile, porcelain pavers, or other
vitrified tiles—all fired at extremely
high temperatures—are best able to tolerate rapid changes in temperature
without cracking. The same tiles are
suitable for surrounding a wood-burn-

ing stove. Unglazed tile used as a fireback will blacken over
time, but glazed products can usually be cleaned of soot.
Masonry and refractory mortar used for firebricks and
masonry-supply grout are essential components of a proper
installation.

## DECORATIVE ACCENTS

Beyond the conventions of foyers and fireplaces, tile enters a
more whimsical realm. Properly used, it has the ability to accentuate the positive and cover up the unfortunate. A beautiful
roundel window becomes a more important focal point when
ringed with tile; a column ornamented with mosaics is even
more dramatic. Call attention to a window seat with a border of
tile marking its edges and lining the wall beneath it. On the
other hand, the plainest plaster walls or the roughest window
openings, adorned with brightly colored tiles, assume a graphic
power. Tile borders and trims can add the complex detail that
is sadly lacking in most contemporary construction. In an environment of hollow-core doors and gypsum board walls, tile
deployed as a crown molding or baseboard can be an effective
stand-in for fine plaster or wood detailing.

Eye-catching tile is particularly effective at defining transitions—of both planes and architectural elements. That's why
even a simple tile floor border or baseboard is so visually satisfy-
ing. Where wall meets ceiling is an even more visible location for
tile in lieu of, or in addition to, cove molding. For double the
impact, run one row of tile at the bottom and another at the top
of a wall. A frieze applied high on the wall or above a window can

draw attention to a high ceiling or fill a
lifeless area above windows. Even ceilings can be improved with tile, by, for
example, defining the area over a window seat or accenting beams with a border of tile. (Be sure proper installation
methods are used to ensure a firm
bond.) Other rich accent areas are
around door and window openings,
where a border of one or more tiles can
add instant personality to a room.
Framed in tile, a featureless door can
rise above its mundane origins to serve
as a deliberately simple foil to the surrounding ornament.

To accent either doors or windows:

• Use slim "liners" for a subtle effect, or turn them on
their sides and mix colors for drama.

• Build up several rows of coordinated or deliberately
disparate borders for a bold gesture.

• Outline openings in triangles of tile laid with a flat edge
abutting the frame.

• Build up tile arches over door and window openings if
ceiling height allows.

• Align windows and doors of uneven heights with a tile
treatment of consistent height.

Tiles set around the window frame may be purely decorative, but they can also actually meet the sash itself and eliminate the need for a wood frame and sill. Tiled sills form an easy-to-clean surface beneath house plants. Proper trim pieces will give such an installation a polished appearance and ensure that only glazed surfaces are exposed to water. When using any tile detail at windows, you'll probably want to eliminate fabric treatments altogether or stick to shirred curtains, matchstick blinds, or some equally simple arrangement for light control and privacy.

## FINAL TOUCHES

Tile can also stand in for conventional furniture. The tradition of tiled furnishings started with French craftsmen in the mid-1700s during the reign of Louis XV, but it was the British Victorians who embraced such ornamentation with a characteristic lack of restraint. Elaborately carved buffets, desks, chairbacks, and even pianos emblazoned with tile were exhibited at London's Great Exhibition of 1851; simpler pieces graced middle-class homes.

Framed out and sheathed in plywood, platforms, benches, and banquettes can be covered with tiles. (For sustained periods of sitting, you'll want to add pads or pillows.) Tiled niches and shelves are relatively easy to create, and are both handy and attractive in kitchens and baths as well as elsewhere. Whether built-in or freestanding, tabletops and buffets lend themselves to ceramic adornment. On wrought iron or steel bases, tile-topped coffee tables, sofa tables, and end tables are handsome additions to any room. Such pieces arc available at one-of-a-kind furniture shops, often in *pique assiette,* but can also be made by anyone with a creative bent. Adorn a tag-sale find, an old Parsons table, or even a twig table with a tile top. Or mount your design on plywood or cementitious backer board and commission a metalsmith to craft a base and frame for your creation.

**OPPOSITE:** A deep baseboard of irregularly glazed handmade tile provides an appropriate footing for eclectic furnishings. **LEFT, TOP TO BOTTOM:** Elephant, tree, and chicken tiles glazed in copper luster and inset in plaster mark the ceiling line in a dressing room. Hand-painted aquatic tiles interspersed with solid-color rectangles and topped with ceramic mosaics serve as an appropriate bathroom baseboard. Glass mosaics add a filigree of detail to a column—one of four—in a bedroom.

Bedrooms also offer possibilities for tile. Cubes tiled on the tops and three sides make admirable bedside tables. Almost any plain mirror can get a new lease on life with an attractive tiled frame. Even a headboard can be treated to tile.

In recent years, truly antique and merely old tiles have become highly collectible. (See Antique and Old Tiles in the Directory of Resources, page 193.) Whether seventeenth-century tin-glazed delft, nineteenth-century English transferware, exquisitely glazed Arts and Crafts pieces, or contemporary pieces you love but can't use in quantity, tiles beg to be displayed. Traditionally such collections were inset as fireplace surrounds, but try out some of these ideas as well:

- Line tiles up on the shelves of a Welsh dresser or on display ledges with a lip designed to hold them safely in place.

- Tile the surface and back of a built-in sideboard or a freestanding country piece.

- Hang individual tiles on the wall using tension-wire plate hangers. Group them for impact, perhaps in an asymmetrical arrangement.

- Use plexiglass, metal, or wooden plate holders to display tiles with compatible objects.

- Mount four tiles on plywood or foam board in a frame with flush edges that will not obscure the design. (The weight of more than four tiles may require professional framing.)

- Display tiles on a plate rail shelf.

- Mix arrangements of old or antique tiles with pottery of the same era, or simply with pieces of compatible spirit.

- "Float" individual tiles in frames to dress up flat or recessed-panel cupboard doors.

- Use old tiles as the centerpiece for a tabletop framed by compatible new ones.

- Use soffits, nooks and crannies, and stairwells to display tile that might be lost on a large expanse of wall.

**BELOW:** A wainscot bordered in Talisman's relief tile depicting spirals and waves steps up the wall to become a headboard. **OPPOSITE:** By hand-painting factory tile bisque "blanks," ceramic artist Marion Grebow transformed a featureless breakfast nook into a perennial spring garden with a tile mural that stretches up to the ceiling.

## Picture a Mural

Murals lend themselves admirably to large expanses of wall or floor, but a mural need not be large—think of a classic four-tile fruit basket on a range hood. Unlike most decorated tiles, which carry a self-contained design, tiles made specifically for murals are designed to be part of a larger whole. They may have geometric, abstract, floral, or other naturalistic themes. Some create a repetitive pattern, such as the traditional Dutch tile, which has a corner treatment designed to provide the link among contiguous tiles. Other murals are made up of tiles that are integral components of an overall scheme, such as a landscape.

A mural may occupy an entire wall or be set into a field of solid-color tile or an overall pattern. When used against field tile, the mural is often outlined with a border for clear definition. Murals make marvelous focal points in rooms without other strong architectural features.

Tile murals work best wherever a large expanse of space offers creative license. In an area without a view or a window, a mural can provide a visual escape hatch by creating the illusion of space beyond. A mural in a window frame can playfully suggest a favorite view. You can work with a tile artist for a one-of-a-kind image or purchase a ready-made mural at a tile dealer.

Often small murals made of antique tiles are inset in a field of compatible contemporary tiles. Original delft tiles, for example, could be surrounded by handmade white squares of the same size, or a blue border could contain the antique pieces within the white field. When using antique tiles, you may want to mount them on plywood so that you can easily take them with you when you move. Simply stow away enough of the surrounding field so that you can fill in the hole left when you remove the mural.

# 7

# The Great Outdoors

*For all its interior possibilities, ceramic tile originated as an exterior cladding material. Ample architectural evidence proves its ability to withstand time and the elements. The Ishtar Gate of ancient Babylon, dating to the sixth century* B.C., *was faced with tile work that survives to this day. Since the twelfth century, tiles have adorned the facades of mosques throughout the Islamic world. The Persian imperial city of Isfahan glitters with blue and turquoise tiles applied more than three centuries ago. When the Moors invaded Spain in 711, they set about cladding interior and exterior walls in Seville, Granada, and other cities with marvelously intricate tile mosaics. Tile fountains in the sumptuous gardens of Granada's Alhambra have been exposed to wind and water for five centuries, but their beauty endures unscathed.*

Italy is also full of outdoor tile applications, often as an integral component of garden design. In the garden behind the church of Santa Chiara in Naples, columns and benches covered in eighteenth-century hand-painted tiles depict flowers and landscapes. To the south, more recently built buildings in Vietri sul Mare sport playful murals of flowers, fruits, people, and animals. But no nation has embraced tiles more passionately than Portugal, where painted tiles emblazoned facades, courtyards, door frames, benches, staircases, and garden architecture from the sixteenth century on. Lisbon is particularly famous for its large-scale exterior use of blue-and-white and polychrome tile murals.

In the Arts and Crafts era, architects used tiles freely outside. Roof tiles were common in Mediterranean-influenced homes, and tile work was often integrated into the facade and nearby walls, perhaps adorning a stone chimney or forming a medallion over an entry.

Today ceramic artists like Shel Neymark celebrate their craft by covering the exteriors of their homes with elaborate tile designs. Stucco, cement, and adobe are natural surfaces for exterior tile installations; other siding materials may first require the application of waterproof plywood or another suitable substrate. In most climates, only tiles rated frost-resistant would be suitable.

Outdoors as well as in, the beauty of tile is hardly dependent upon sheer volume. In fact, most contemporary uses make tile an accent rather than the primary feature. Sensitive ceramic tile detailing can add interest to even the most basic architecture. Windows and doors trimmed in tile, a look that is particularly effective with stucco construction, can make a mundane

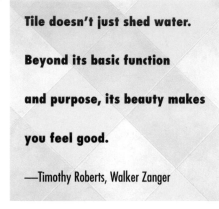

> **Tile doesn't just shed water. Beyond its basic function and purpose, its beauty makes you feel good.**
>
> —Timothy Roberts, Walker Zanger

**PRECEDING PAGES, LEFT:** Yellow octagonal tiles—accented with blue "dots"—on a patio table and a terra-cotta floor of squares, similarly adorned, share an compatible aesthetic. **CENTER:** An inset of hand-painted tiles announces the street number, while acknowledging Florida's native fauna. **RIGHT:** Walker Zanger's Caribbean-style border hails from Italy. **ABOVE:** Designer Van-Martin Rowe accentuated key architectural features of a classic Spanish-style house with a frosting of multicolor tiles, applied to the scratch coat of stucco to sit flush with the finished surface. **OPPOSITE:** Miami's Arquitectonica used bright blue tile around windows and the front door of a stucco house, treating each opening differently.

**Opposite, Above:** The pheasant fountain, made of 1920s Malibu tile, spouts water from a vase that was also part of the original production line. **Opposite, Below:** A fountain and flanking benches display numerous Tunisian tile designs. **Above:** Trickling water, dappled sunshine, anodized metal, and Spanish-style tile work their magic in a Miami courtyard.

and boxlike dwelling special. Just imagine the difference made by enclosing a row of plain windows with a zigzag border of tiles. Tile can also add color, glamour, even mystery to suburban architecture and landscaping. Tile risers on a garden stairway, for instance, add instant ambience.

These suggestions merely scratch the surface of tile's alfresco design possibilities. In regions where the growing season is short, colorful tile accents make the landscape attractive year-round. Pave a terrace or walkway with tile and it takes on a decorative quality that mere wooden decking or concrete cannot possibly provide. Enhance such focal points as an outdoor fireplace or a fountain with decorative tiles. Benches, tables, and planters are logical candidates for tile work, as are spas and pools. Announce your passion for tile at your front door, perhaps in the form of a "doormat" made

from broken pieces of tile or a plaque announcing your name or street number. The right tile is a practical choice around barbecues because it resists grease spills.

## THE RIGHT STUFF

The tradition of defining and embellishing outdoor spaces with ceramic tile has historically been linked to climate. Denizens of the south, whether the Mediterranean countries or Mexico and Florida, perceive tile as a perfectly natural patio and terrace covering; however, such uses in Britain or the northern United States are uncommon. In reality, tile is able to withstand cold weather as well as it does hot. Many high-fired ceramics—both glazed and unglazed—can be used outdoors if properly installed. The issue isn't so much one of climate as it is temperature changes that cause freeze-thaw cycles from night to day.

**Top:** Each stair riser exhibits a different pattern of tiny glass tiles, which also cover paired urns and form a numbered plaque. **Above Left:** A long staircase displays just some of the numerous Malibu designs still available, interspersed with high-fired terra-cotta tiles, which also serve as risers. **Above Right:** A Moroccan staircase uses one pattern on risers, another on steps. **Opposite:** Randomly placed blue and green tiles are a cooling influence in a southern California location.

**RIGHT:** Designer Dennis Jenkins makes a major tile statement at the entry of his own house in Coconut Grove. Shimmering shards of broken tile add impact to the columns.
**ABOVE:** A tile address plaque on a checkerboard "fragment" alerts the mailman. The two tarot card tiles are Spanish, the mounted prince, Turkish.

Unless you live in a climate where the temperature never drops below freezing, tile must be rated frost-resistant, to meet certain standards established by the American Society for Testing & Materials. Tile used on patios and walkways also must be slip-resistant and have a high abrasion factor. Slip resistance is particularly crucial around pools and stairs. Frost-resistant porcelain, quarry tile, and some terra-cotta and glazed tiles may meet all these criteria. (Certain glazes can be affected by the acids in rain.) Many tiles designed for outdoor use now have abrasive particles applied to the surface before firing to minimize the possibility of slipping. Quarry tile's slightly textured surface also resists slipping, as does textured porcelain; smaller tiles are also safer. It cannot be overstated that the name a tile goes by is less important than the qualities it possesses. When making purchase decisions, tell the retailer how and where you want to install the tile and let him or her steer you toward those that are suitable. Before the actual purchase, ask to see literature confirming that the manufacturer has indeed designated the tile as frost-resistant and suitable for exterior use.

There is considerable debate over the suitability of terra cotta for exterior use. Again, the dispute may in large part be due to terminology. Low-fired tiles don't hold up well outside. And handmade tiles' undulating backs require an installation that compensates for their irregularity. If you want the look of terra cotta, don't say you want a terra-cotta tile. Instead, tell a salesperson that you want a tile that looks like terra cotta but can be used outside.

## PROPER INSTALLATION

Choosing a suitable tile is not the only factor necessary for successful outdoor use. What goes underneath and on top of the tile is equally important. Just as the tile must be frost-resistant, so must the mortar and grout and the installation itself be able to handle changes in temperature.

Major exterior installations are usually handled by professional tile and masonry contractors, but it is still important to understand what is involved. Proper underlayment is crucial.

Courtyards, walkways, and patios at grade should be laid on a concrete slab placed over a bed of crushed stone or gravel. The gravel bed allows any water than has penetrated the tile and the concrete to disperse into the soil below. A thick-bed installation method is essential for cracked or damaged surfaces; sometimes thin-set can be used over existing masonry that is in excellent condition. New areas such as courtyards and patios can be thin- or thick-set on a concrete slab placed over a bed of gravel. The surface must be sloped toward drains and provided with properly spaced expansion joints. A similar approach should be used on terraces and balconies, with the addition of a waterproof membrane to protect against water leakage to the space below.

Standing water is the enemy of exterior tile installations. Even a slight hollow or depression will keep water from draining, as will an accumulation of leaves or other debris. The water will eventually find its way to the nearest hairline crack, and when the temperature drops, it will freeze and expand, opening up the cracks. Even differences between daytime and nighttime temperatures can cause contraction and expansion, as do the extremes of temperature between seasons. Since fine cracks inevitably will form, it is essential that the installation minimize water entry by sloping all surfaces toward a drain.

In addition, expansion joints filled with a flexible material must be installed to allow the tiles to expand and contract slightly without breaking. Measuring from ⅜ inch to ½ inch or more, expansion joints are filled with silicone, polysulfide, or, most commonly, urethane. Temperature and climate will affect their positioning, but typically they are placed at least every 16 feet (12 feet is preferable), around columns and piping, and at all walls. It's worth mentioning that the use of expansion joints is mandated by the Tile Council of America and by local building codes. Their placement is the responsibility of the architect; whenever possible, the placement of joints should be incorporated into the design of the surface.

Portland-cement or latex-portland-cement grout will perform well unless salt and chemicals are likely to be used on the

**ABOVE:** A concrete bench treated to a *pique assiette* veneer is right at home surrounded by the lush foliage of a tropical garden. **LEFT:** In another lesson in the powerful impact that even a small use of tile can provide in an architectural setting, four squares in a Moorish pattern are inset diagonally into a stucco wall. A painted border, reiterated in the window surround below, is a nice example of mixed media, complemented by Mother Nature's own contribution. **BELOW:** An array of original Malibu tiles frame an arched doorway at the Adamson House in Malibu. **OPPOSITE:** A rainbow of Moroccan cement tiles laid in a random pattern brightens up a tiny terrace in Provence.

**LEFT:** A recirculating waterfall spills over a mosaic mural of colorful tile—some broken into rubble—and anodized copper, designed by painter Debra Yates, into a Coconut Grove swimming pool. **ABOVE:** Four antique English tiles find a new and unusual home framed in a painted fence around a Florida patio.

surface to melt ice. In any case, salts from deicers should be removed from tile surfaces promptly to avoid a crusty residue.

Recommendations on sealing unglazed tile in exterior situations vary from manufacturer to manufacturer. While it does add a measure of protection, any sealant will need to be reapplied from time to time. A buildup of several coats may require removal before a fresh coat is applied. Most tile manufacturers recommend specific sealants and procedures for their products. Others recommend that no sealant be used. Always ask for the manufacturer's specific instructions.

## POOLS AND SPAS

Pools and spas may require vitrified tiles. For safety reasons, tile used around pools and as steps in pools and spas should always be slip-resistant; glazed tiles can become too slick when wet unless they have a special abrasive surface or texture. Coping, used at the juncture of the pool wall and the horizontal decking, may be made of precast concrete or bullnose bricks; however, tile coping is the most handsome alternative, particularly when used with matching patio tile. Inside the pool itself, the combination of glazed tile, rippling water, and sunshine creates a magical, inviting effect.

Tile can be used in several ways in a pool or spa. Four to 6 inches of waterline tile adds an attractive touch to any instal-

## Pool Basics

Although in theory tile can be added to a pool that is being resurfaced, normally tile is installed when a pool is built. In order to support tile, the pool must be made of concrete. The concrete surface should be finished with a medium-rough bush-hammer finish or with the aggregate exposed.

Before tile work begins, your pool contractor will ascertain that there is no leakage by filling the pool with water to see if there is a significant drop in water level after a period of time. The surface is then sealed with a waterproof membrane. Some membranes involve the use of portland-cement mortar with metal lath; others require direct setting of the tile into the membrane.

**ABOVE:** At one end of a Miami swimming pool, a waterfall is backed with a harlequin design crafted of glass mosaic tiles, which also appear at the pool's waterline. **OPPOSITE:** On a stucco wall shielding a pool from the Los Angeles streets an undulating mosaic of broken tile crafted by Projectile draws its subject matter from nearby shimmering water and graceful grasses. Four rows of blue glazed tiles trim the edge of the pool.

lation, but it is actually also highly functional: The glazed surface reduces the buildup of scum and mineral deposits that are left when the water level recedes. Tile may continue all the way down the sides and onto the floor of the pool, although there its purpose is primarily decorative; more commonly, except for the waterline area, the rest of the pool is plastered. Seats and steps may also be tiled.

Only tiles recommended by manufacturers as suitable for pools should be used. Some are glazed in either a matte or a glossy finish; in the case of unglazed porcelain, the color extends through the body of the tile. (Tile used on a pool or spa floor, steps, or built-in seating should have a matte finish.) In addition to their ability to withstand impact, pool tiles are acid-resistant and will not tarnish or fade. Six-inch square pool tile is standard, but there are many of other sizes and shapes, from 1-inch mosaics up to 12-inch squares. Square tiles work well on rectangular pools, but narrow rectangles (6 by 1¾ inches, for example) or ceramic mosaics can navigate curved surfaces better. Smaller tiles

are usually mounted on paper or mesh or dot-mounted to ease installation in general and specifically on curved surfaces. Glass mosaics may be used as well, and can be highly resistant to chemicals, acids, fading, and frost. Because of their expense, they are most often used as waterline trim or in small pools and spas.

Turquoise blue has been the traditional color choice for water installations because it masks mineral deposits, which are revealed more quickly on dark colors; textured, patterned, or mottled light shades also tend to hide them better. Fish and nautical motifs are popular for symbolic reasons. Moorish designs have traditionally been used around pools, but today a variety of colors and abstract and geometric designs are available. Custom designs can also be commissioned.

Tile used for pools usually must be frost-resistant, which also means that it has a dense glaze. (Some non-frost-resistant pool tiles are made for use in tropical climates.) With high absorptive or other inappropriate tile, the water could eventually work its way through the tile and cause it to discolor or loosen. No matter

**ABOVE:** A tiled potting and flower-arranging area easily wipes clean. The glazed tiles were imported from Tunisia in the early twentieth century. **OPPOSITE:** Talavera tiles step up the side of a staircase, an extension of the classic treatment used on the risers.

how reputable your pool contractor, it wouldn't hurt to doublecheck with the manufacturer to confirm that the tiles are suitable for a pool in your climate, ensuring the permanence of the installation.

Given the cost of tiling an entire pool, a spa is a far more likely site in which to go all out. In fact, if you are fortunate enough to have both, one approach is to tile the spa entirely and then use a related accent treatment in the pool. Tile can transform a spa from a primarily functional backyard feature into the focal point of a garden. For example, a small fountain can serve as a backdrop for the spa, linked with a similar tile treatment.

In addition to a border of tile, you can customize a pool or spa with tile in the following ways:

- Inset tiles randomly in the floor or walls.

- Incorporate a wall of tile above the pool into the design or use it as the backdrop for a pump-operated waterfall.
- Line a water slide from spa to pool.
- Build a shallow bench in the pool and tile it to match the waterline treatment.

Books on the architecture of Mexico, Morocco, Turkey, Portugal, and other countries with strong ceramic traditions provide a rich source of exterior uses. In the United States, Miami, Santa Fe, San Antonio, Pasadena, Detroit, Kansas City, and Santa Barbara have all preserved examples of early-twentieth-century—and sometimes older—tile work, providing a wealth of ideas that can be adapted to contemporary use. The subways of New York prove that inspiration is everywhere.

**ABOVE:** Designer Fernando Sanchez created a lotus flower mosaic of old roof tiles, antique terra cotta, and marble chips in the courtyard of a Miami house. **OPPOSITE:** New terra-cotta tiles, their lichen dusting hinting at an ancient lineage, define an outdoor shower. **OVERLEAF:** A tiled niche shelters Hindu goddess Saraswati.

Success with ceramic tile involves practical as well as aesthetic matters. Whether your project is small or large, whether you design it or hire a professional, and whether you install it yourself or rely on a tile setter, you should be aware of certain facts before purchasing tile. This section covers the ins and outs of working with installers, designers, and tile salespersons; selecting the right tile for your job; ideas for tile patterns you may want to copy or build upon; and tips on how to judge an installation. Also included are pointers on care and maintenance, a glossary of terms, a list of books for additional information, and a list of tile artists, dealers, manufacturers, and some specialized sources. When it comes to installation, simple tile jobs can often be handled by a competent do-it-yourselfer. (A list of instructional books and videos follows.) Basic materials can be purchased at any tile supplier and tile cutters and other tools can be rented.

DESIGN WORKBOOK

# PATTERN PLAY

One of the best ways to express your creativity with tile is to play with patterns formed by one or more shapes and colors. Even working with a single tile color and shape, it is possible to create a range of patterns (see examples, pages 196 to 199).

Square tiles allow the most options. From a simple grid to a staggered or diagonal placement to an instep pattern that combines a small and a larger square, the arrangement can be manipulated endlessly. Rectangles can also produce diverse effects, from a staggered brick look to a double or single herringbone to more complex basketweave or parquet-like patterns. Diamonds can combine to create stars or hexagons. Triangles provide wonderful opportunities for chevrons, zigzags, stripes, and pinwheels. Tiles can also be cut to create more pattern possibilities. A rectangle yields two triangles, for example. But avoid cutting pillowed tiles to make patterns since thickness varies across the face of the tile.

## MIXING SHAPES

A few shapes require a mate. For example, an Ottoman star cannot work without a companion cross. The irregular octagon (really a square with clipped corners) is often used with a small square inset, called a dot. But most shapes can be mixed with other shapes for ultimate flexibility; for example, four elongated hexagons (also known as lozenges or pickets) can enclose a square, or rectangles can band a

square, the corners marked with a dot. Decorative trim pieces expand the galaxy of available shapes. Some, such as thin rectangular liners, can be used in a variety of ways against field tile or with other geometrically shaped accent pieces. Some ideas on how to combine shapes follow:

- Surround each square with four thin liners to form a dynamic grid.
- Use squares and triangles to create an argyle effect.
- Introduce pairs of triangles into a field of squares.
- Intersperse narrow liners randomly in a field of square tiles. Just be sure to use the same number of liners in each row to make them come out evenly.

## MIXING COLORS

When you add the element of different colors, the possibilities are multiplied, from simple contrasting borders to patchwork designs and "plaids." Inspirations for tile patterns are everywhere, whether in an Amish quilt, a Native American motif, or a Florentine courtyard. You can use these classic patterns and modern adaptations as the jumping-off point for designing your own patterns. Sometimes a simple change can make even a basic design special. For example:

- Run a checkerboard on the diagonal.
- Use two colors of triangular tiles to form an angled, lattice pattern.
- Intersperse a second color of quarry tile every three or five tiles, offsetting the rows.

If you are attracted to such designs, plot them out on graph paper, using colored pencils, or cut "tiles" from colored construction paper and lay them out on the floor. Such tools can

## Installation Aesthetics

Tile, particularly handmade varieties, is not perfectly flat; and pillowed tiles, whether factory- or handmade, slope to the edges rather like a flattened pillow. To some degree, an installation should allow you to sense the tile's thickness and unevenness. The job should never be so perfect that the tile looks like scored laminate or solid surfacing. A good installer walks the thin line between neatness and bland consistency. This almost always involves some tradeoffs to make tiles of a certain size fit an existing wall or floor.

Highly visible areas, such as around the sink or where you put on makeup or talk on the phone, are of primary importance. For a project of any complexity, the tile setter will probably lay out the tile on the floor before beginning the job. The purpose of this dry run is twofold. It determines where cuts should be made; it also allows handmade or other irregularly shaded tiles to be arranged in an attractive, apparently random fashion. Moreover, machine-made tiles with a silk-screen design that mimics marble or another natural finish can be placed in a way that will disguise their limited variation.

prove helpful before you go to a tile dealer. Or buy a few tiles of different colors and play with them until you come up with an appealing pattern. You may even want to mount sample tiles on plywood, using Velcro tabs to hold them in place.

## FROM PURCHASE TO INSTALLATION

Ceramic tile is practically ubiquitous, available at home centers, hardware stores, flooring outlets, tile distributors, and specialty tile shops. (Check your local Yellow Pages for listings under *Tile-Ceramic-Dealers.*) A professional designer can gain you entrée to "to the trade only" sources that stock unusual, often handmade or specialty, tile.

Visits to showrooms are an essential part of planning a tile installation. Hundreds if not thousands of samples will be on display, along with idea-provoking installations. Notice how one tile is laid end to end as a wainscot and above it is installed on the diagonal; how a smaller version of a tile used in the tub area can subtly define the sink area; or how trim pieces can expand the potential of any design. Observe that all four walls in a room needn't be treated in an identical fashion for a coherent look and how tile can be used to create a focal point or highlight several areas.

### What to Expect from a Retailer

Wherever you shop, remember that a salesperson's job is to sell tile. While some give good design advice—salespeople at high-end specialty shops are the most apt to have a design background—don't assume that all have aesthetic training. On the other hand, you *should* expect technical knowledge. If you don't get it, go elsewhere. On the West Coast you are likely to find sellers who have completed a program as Certified Tile Consultants. This means that they have been in the business at least three years and have demonstrated knowledge of building and plumbing codes, blueprint reading, manufacturing standards, and installation methods. Any good retailer should be able to field technical questions, but since the level of knowledge varies greatly from individual to individual, it is important to also ask for manufacturers' literature on the products you are considering. If the retailer can't provide it, contact the manufacturer.

Tile dealers or discounters may offer closeout styles and colors at attractive prices; home centers also have good prices, but selection is generally limited to fairly standard choices. Neither is likely to have the kind of inspiring vignettes you'll find in tile showrooms and specialty shops. Larger outfits will have more products and are less likely to charge for special shipping. Those serviced by a local distributor network can often get special orders delivered more quickly.

Do your homework before you go, explain where and how you plan to use the tile, and be straightforward about your budget. If you are willing to go all out on wall tile, but are determined to save on floor tile, say so up front. In a sense, the salesperson's role is to eliminate options. A motivated seller may ask about your favorite architectural styles, personal tastes, and living habits. Finding out whether you have kids or live by the beach or in a restored Victorian will help the seller rule out unsuitable options immediately, enabling you to zero in on real possibilities. The bottom line is that you should buy from someone who is responsive to your needs and not just eager to dispose of inventory.

### Making a Selection

Once you have narrowed your choices, buy a few samples. Many tile showrooms will allow you to borrow samples for a small deposit. When you are selecting tiles from a catalog and cannot feel the texture and experience the color and quality of the glaze, ask for samples before committing yourself. Live with them for a few days and look at them next to the other surfaces and materials they will share the space with. Be sure to switch on the lights in the room the tile will inhabit. Often tile color will look different in your home than it did under showroom lights.

## TIME TO ORDER

When you are ready to buy tile, it is essential that you purchase the right amount of field tile and proper trim pieces at the same time. Tiles are packed in cartons that usually contain up to 12 square feet of tile, although mounted mosaic tiles and others may be packed in boxes that hold up to 20 square feet. Decorative trim and borders usually sell by the linear foot, and specialty pieces such as corners and borders, by the piece. However, you may prefer to leave calculations to professionals, especially if you are using more than one tile or creating an intricate pattern.

If you are working with an architect or interior designer, he or she will specify exactly which pieces are needed. For a complex job, the designer may even take elevation drawings to the tile retailer and have them reviewed by store personnel before the order is finalized.

If you are doing the installation yourself, bring exact measurements and a detailed drawing or a set of blueprints to the showroom so that a salesperson can specify the order. If you are using a professional to install your design, let him or her be "the responsible party." If the tile setter handles the order, you will avoid any finger-pointing midjob if a shortage of tiles or a missing trim piece results in a delay. Since an installer may overorder to be sure of having sufficient material on hand, it is not a bad idea to get two opinions. Check the installer's order against what the salesperson says you need. Or simply say, "My installer says I need this much. Do you agree?"

Most professionals advise that you buy 5 to 10 percent more tile than you actually need to cover breakage and cuts during installation and to replace the occasional tile broken at a later date. If the design is complex, laid on the diagonal, or will involve an unusual amount of cutting, order even more. Some retailers will allow full cases of tiles to be returned for cash or credit. Custom-made or special-order tile usually cannot be returned. Check before ordering. If the tile is not in stock but is a commonly ordered design, it is likely to be warehoused by a local distributor, and delivery should take no longer than a week to ten days. Custom orders and imported tile may take up to eight weeks, or even longer, to arrive; custom colors can also prolong the ordering process.

## FINAL INSPECTION AND BEYOND

Before leaving the store with your tile order, be sure to inspect every box for variations and damage. Tile is a natural product, so there is a certain amount of variation from run to run. Ideally, all your tile should be from the same shade lot. (Good lighting during installation is also essential to ensure proper matching of color and design.)

Be sure to keep copies of invoices plus the name of the manufacturer, style, and color of the tile. Importers will sometimes use their own labels or give a foreign tile a name of their own, so check the packing carton against the invoice. The invoice is also useful if there are any claims for defects that turn up after installation.

## FIGURING THE COST

Prices for tile cover a broad spectrum. You should be able to find remaindered or odd lots for as little as $1 a square foot, a clever strategy if you are mixing colors and designs. For full-price tiles, expect to pay from $2 on up to $50 a square foot; hand-painted or imported pieces could run as high as

$200 a square foot. Complex designs, custom painting, glass insets, and other special effects also increase the tab. Solid-color squares are usually more affordable than textured, relief, or hand-painted designs, larger sizes, and unusual shapes. Some handmade tiles are priced individually rather than by the square foot.

The field tile cost is the result of multiplying the cost per square foot by the number of square feet needed (including overage). To that, add the cost of trim pieces. Figuring the cost of installation is more complicated. As for any tradesperson's work, get at least three estimates and be sure that prices are based on the same methods of installation and materials. Labor cost will vary depending upon the area in which you live and the complexity of the project, which in turn affects the time required. Typically, large areas of flat tile will cost less per square foot than smaller jobs that entail a lot of detail and trim work. The more cuts required to fit tile around corners and into odd-shaped places, the higher labor costs will run. Likewise, diagonal patterns need more cuts

and cost more than a straight course. Many installers charge more for handmade tile, as its irregularities make it more time-consuming to lay.

You might have to pay at least as much for the underlayment, adhesive, and labor required to install the tile as you do for the tile itself. Generally, covering a countertop with tile will cost more than installing laminate and less than solid surfacing. Tile floors tend to cost more than most resilient sheet flooring and are usually comparable to the cost of hardwood floors.

## PROFESSIONAL ASSISTANCE

An attractive tile job depends equally upon excellent design and proper installation. It's important to understand the roles that designers and architects, store personnel, and installers can play in helping you achieve satisfactory results. Within the various professions, there is often considerable overlap: The best designers understand the technical limitations of tile; the best installers are artists in their own right.

Architects, interior designers, decorators, and kitchen and bath designers have all been trained to work with tile,

## A Good Job

Before hiring an installer, check out a few of his or her completed projects. At its most basic, the object of an installation is to cut the tiles to fit the space, without interfering with the pattern of each tile or the composition itself. Straight grout lines and clean cuts are a given. An installer should plan the layout to locate cut tiles in a place that will hide any lack of trueness in the walls.

When evaluating an installation, here's what else to look for:
• Assess the overall look. Is the work neat? Don't assume that a jarring design is the installer's fault. You may simply not like the tile itself.
• Are exterior corners handled neatly?
• Is the corner where the installation begins and ends handled well?
• How about transitions from tile to plaster or other surfaces?
• Do grout lines fall in a pleasing fashion? How about

where field tile meets a border or where tiles of different sizes meet?
• If the pattern is centered on a wall or floor, is it properly balanced?
• Are sight lines upon entering the room taken into consideration?
• Are cut tiles handled neatly? You shouldn't see narrow slivers on one side of the room. Most walls are off square, and small pieces of tile will be obvious when the wall is not true. Slivers also may loosen over time.
• Were other cuts made in the least obtrusive places?
• With handmade tiles, were machine cuts roughed up with sandpaper or a piece of tile so that the new straight edges match the uncut edges of whole tiles?
• Does the design (if any) carry neatly around corners? Cove pieces provide a neat and durable corner treatment in showers, instead of simply butting tiles.
• Are there cracks? If so, ask the homeowners if the installer advised beefing up the floor but they had declined to spend the extra money.

but each approaches design from a different perspective. While interior designers and architects are sensitive to all aspects of design, not all kitchen and bath designers have such broad training and may lack the aesthetic sensibility to make the most of tile. Nor is every interior designer or architect particularly creative with tile. If you aren't excited by the tile ideas generated by a professional who has proven satisfactory for the rest of a job, you might want to hire another designer as tile consultant.

Some specialty tile retailers have experts on staff to assist homeowners with design. Typically, there is no charge for  this service. A small job, like a backsplash or a mudroom floor, doesn't usually require a designer. But it is advisable to use the services of a design professional on a large job to integrate tile work into the overall scheme. The designer will usually supervise the installer, troubleshooting ordering and execution so that nothing is left to chance. Some will approve the tile layout after it has been dry-laid on the floor; others will draw up a blueprint of the tile pattern for the installer. A designer or general contractor will schedule the various trades in a timely fashion, ensuring that the plumber, for example, has completed the necessary work before the tile setter arrives.

## FINDING AN INSTALLER

There are various ways to find a quality tile installer, in part depending on the scope of your project. Most designers and architects have ongoing relationships with installers and will vouch for their quality. Tile showroom managers will often provide a list of installers, although they may refer people who purchase a lot of material at their stores rather than those whose work they know. If you are working directly with a general contractor, make sure his or her installer is one whose work you have seen and like. The Yellow Pages lists tile contractors under *Tile-Ceramic-Contractors*. National tile associations, such as the Ceramic Tile Institute of America, and the National Tile Contractors Association (see Associations, page 194) and local chapters of tile contractors' associations can also make recommendations. In most areas, tile contractors need not be certified. Use a job contract to clarify all components of an installation, including compliance with local building codes and the methods established by the Tile Council of America, as outlined in its *Handbook for Ceramic Tile Installation* (see page 195 to order). Be wary of general contractors or handymen who claim that they install tile. A good carpenter is not necessarily skilled in tile work.

If you are contracting the job yourself, it is essential that you interview several tile setters, see their work, and check references. Ask former clients about the installer's cleanliness, timeliness, courtesy, and price. Be sure to visit not only recently completed jobs but also one that has been in place for a couple of years—by which time problems are likely to have cropped up. The jobs should be similar in scope to yours and feature similar tile. If you are using handmade tile and all you see are factory tile jobs, the installer may not be comfortable with the challenges of handmade materials. For a job of any complexity, sketches of the design will prove a valuable communication tool. When comparing bids, be aware that a low price may mean that the installer plans to take shortcuts such as simply filling a small space with grout instead of taking the time to cut tile.

Once you have made your selection, continue to keep the lines of communication open. If you have selected the right person, he or she will be as eager as you to do a quality job. A good tile installer works things out in advance. Unless the manufacturer specifically states otherwise, have the installer shuffle the tiles from different boxes to assure the natural variations that add to tile's appeal. Ask your installer's advice and make your preferences clear, including how to treat grout. If you have any doubts about the tile itself, voice them now; a manufacturer will not entertain claims after installation unless there is a technical failure. While it is preferable to be at home when the job is being done so you are available for last-minute questions, let the installer do the job without hanging over him or her.

## AN INSTALLATION PRIMER

Simple tile installations can often be handled by do-it-yourselfers, but others require the experience and skill of a professional. After spending good money for a quality product, it is folly to risk spoiling it with poor craftsmanship or an inadequate substrate. Unless you are planning to lay the tile yourself, it is not essential that you know all the intricacies of installation; still, an understanding of certain basics can influence your choice of tile. In turn, the tile selected will definitely affect the cost of installation. You'll need to ensure that the surface is properly prepared, that the floor below is level and can support the weight

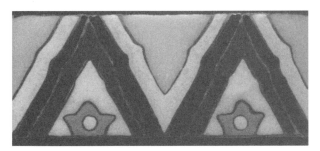

of the tile and mortar, and that there are no structural problems behind the walls. You'll also need to decide how to handle any resultant difference in level between a new area and an adjoining room. Such issues will also affect the type of installation—either thin-set or thick-set—you elect. Finally, if you are planning to seal terra cotta or other unglazed tile, it can usually be done after the tile is set and before it is grouted.

## ASSESSING THE STRUCTURE

Because the weight of tiled floors and walls is substantial, your contractor or tile installer will examine the area in question to ascertain whether it requires additional load-bearing support. He or she may recommend an inspection by an architect or structural engineer to reveal if previous renovations or water damage have affected the structural integrity. If so, it may be necessary to install additional supporting beams below the area to be tiled. You may simply be advised to avoid the use of particularly heavy tile on upper floors or to use only a thin-set installation.

An important flooring consideration is flexibility. Most

## Water Protection

If a tile installation is not well planned and executed, trapped moisture will cause the wall behind to swell, eventually exerting pressure on the tiles, which may pop off or crack. Water can also leak through to the floor below, damaging ceilings and more. The use of a waterproof surface behind tile is essential in bathrooms and other wet areas, as is the use of adhesives and grouts that can withstand constant exposure to moisture. Several materials and techniques are key.

Thick-set installations must have:
- A waterproof backing or membrane on floors, walls, and any areas exposed to water or high temperatures from steam.
- Latex-modified mortars and grouts or epoxies on shower floors.
- A waterproof membrane in any area whose underlying surface is wood or is cracked or otherwise unstable.

Thin-set installations require:
- Cementitious backer board for bathroom walls and other high-moisture areas. Green board can be used in areas not in direct contact with water.
- Sealing all cut edges—including cutouts for plumbing—of cementitious backer board with special waterproof tape.
- Fiberglass-reinforced portland-cement board in areas that meet the tub or under the shower base.
- Cementitious backer board on floors—as well as walls and benches in showers and tubs with showers—attached with water-resistant screws or nails; seams sealed with fiberglass tape, then coated with mortar or epoxy.

residences are constructed with wood joists and wood is inherently a flexible material, meaning that it will give in the center under heavy loads. The greater the distance between supports, the more movement or play there will be in the floor. Tile must be installed over a rigid surface to avoid cracking; the surface cannot deflect more than a minimal amount. For example, a room 10 feet long should not bend more than ⅓ inch in the center. An engineer or architect will ascertain the maximum allowable deflection for the span involved and recommend how to proceed. He or she may advise stabilizing the structure, perhaps by applying a layer of plywood topped with cementitious backer board. Flexible grout and expansion joints—running joints that allow for the hard surface of cement and tile to handle slight movement—may also be required. It's important to state that either a mud-set installation or the use of cementitious backer board cannot compensate for movement in the structure; instead, the underlying structural problems must be addressed.

When it comes to tiling a wall, the first structural consideration is whether it is load-bearing—meaning that it supports the ceiling and other floors above—or non-load-bearing. Unless there is structural damage, load-bearing walls are normally strong enough to support the added weight of either a mud-set or thin-set tile installation, as can walls that are located on a concrete slab or over a beam. Non-load-bearing walls typically cannot handle a thick-set installation unless another joist is added underneath. Otherwise, the added weight may cause sagging, cracking of tile, and even separation where the floor and the wall intersect.

## SURFACE PREPARATION

After any structural concerns have been dealt with, the surface to be tiled must be clean, level, stable, and, if necessary, waterproofed. The most common cause of a poor tile installation is an improperly prepared substrate, which can lead to maintenance headaches, particularly in kitchens and baths where previous plumbing problems may have caused damage or lingering wetness behind the walls.

*Preparing Walls* Wall surfaces must be in good enough condition to enable adhesive to bond. Walls that are severely damaged require a new backing before a thin-set tile installation or the tiles will eventually pop off or crack. Here's what to expect in terms of preparation for various conditions:

- Loose plaster or cement: Remove; patch as necessary.
- Wallcovering: Remove, including glue residue.
- Paint: Remove or scarify by cutting through the surface to release trapped moisture.
- Wood: Nail boards securely; sand to roughen surface. If boards are twisted, cover with ¼-inch plywood, or, better yet, cementitious backer board.
- Laminate: Rough up with sandpaper.
- Dampness: Correct the root problem and patch.
- Cracks: Fill small ones; large cracks require that the underlying structural problem be repaired first.

*Preparing Floors* Often tile can be laid over existing floors. The type of flooring and its condition may determine the method of tile setting. Generally, glossy or painted surfaces should be sanded. Important: Never attempt to remove old flooring that contains asbestos (including some older vinyl-composition products). Instead, call in a professional who will usually recommend covering it with underlayment before tiling. You may have to build up existing floors to provide a level surface. Specific guidelines for various materials follow:

- Wood: Sometimes loose boards can be nailed down securely; if they are twisted or warped, apply the appropriate underlayment, such as plywood, and use the thin-set method. Or, if the floor can handle the weight, use a thick-bed mud base with a waterproof membrane.
- Vinyl or vinyl-composition tiles, sheet vinyl, and linoleum: Make sure that the surface is completely stable and level; then sand or treat it with a degreasing, dewaxing stripper before tiling over it; to level,

use a troweled-on underlayment material.

- Concrete: Usually ideal for either thin- or thick-set installation. Remove paint and any buildup of adhesives remaining from another flooring material; if necessary, use an underlayment for leveling before a thin-set installation. Unevenness or severe cracks must be corrected before installation.
- Terrazzo: Scarify, then treat like concrete.
- Ceramic tile: If level, sound, and properly laid, scarify or etch for proper adhesion and lay new tile over it. Otherwise, remove or secure and use troweled-on underlayment to level. Use a strong bonding agent such as latex-modified mortar or epoxy.
- Carpet: Remove, along with any adhesive; proceed as above depending upon the underlying surface.
- Cushioned sheet vinyl or vinyl composition: Remove, along with any adhesive, proceed as above depending upon the underlying surface.

## ACTUAL INSTALLATION

A tile job can take anywhere from a few hours to several days depending upon the size and complexity of the project and the methods used. Regardless of whether installation is thick-set, thin-set, or a hybrid method—known as medium-set—the process involves bonding the tile to the substrate. Each tile is pressed to the surface with a twisting motion to ensure even bonding, then gently tamped in place with a rubber mallet. Large tiles may need to be "back-buttered," coated with more bonding agent in addition to what is on the surface. A score-and-snap cutter handles straight cuts on most types of tile; a water-cooled electrical tile cutter with a diamond saw blade is needed for finer edges, compound straight cuts, and thicker-bodied tiles. Tile nippers navigate around plumbing and electrical fixtures, or an electric drill with a carborundum bit can cut neat holes. After the area has been tiled, it is left to set for several hours or a couple of days, depending upon the setting material used. Finally, joints are filled with grout.

## THICK-SET OR THIN-SET?

*Thick-set, thick-bed, mud-set,* and *cement-bed* are all terms used to describe a process whereby tiles are "floated," or installed directly in a bed of portland cement, which is reinforced with wire mesh and applied over a curing membrane that isolates the floor below or the wall behind. Alternatively, the tile can be bonded to dry mortar with a bonding agent as in the thin-set technique described below.

The thick-set method was standard until the 1950s, when new products made faster, less labor-intensive techniques possible. A mud-set installation is extremely sound, stable, impervious to water, and can compensate for irregular or unlevel surfaces. Mud-set allows an installer to create a gentle slope, facilitating proper drainage in a shower or correcting a wall that isn't plumb. Despite their advantages, such installations are more expensive, take longer, and add 20 pounds per square foot to the total weight. They also raise the height of a floor (or protrude from the wall) somewhere between ¾ inch and 2 inches, in addition to the thickness of the tile.

In thin-set, tiles are bonded to an existing surface or an applied substrate, or underlayment, with a thin coat of mastic or epoxy applied with a notched trowel. Suitable substrates depend upon location and include exterior-grade plywood, glass-mesh mortar board, or cementitious backer board. Gypsum board (Sheetrock) suffices for walls. Plywood and backer board (brand names include Wonder-

### Back Matter

You will notice differences in the backs of some tiles; these reflect the specific machinery or molds used in production and usually have no bearing on use. Most handmade tiles have ribbed or flat backs; machined ones may display a wafflelike grid, ridges, or some other pattern. A slight pattern may improve bonding since it makes the tile less apt to slide and increases the surface area. On the other hand, proponents of flat backs claim that they bond better to the substrate. Assuming proper installation methods are followed, both types produce fine results. Tiles with raised knobs, known as button backs, require a thicker than usual mortar bed or back-buttering.

Board and Durock) are acceptable for countertops or floors. (See Water Protection on page 175 for special requirements in wet areas.)

A thin-set installation costs less, can be completed more quickly, and cures faster than the thick-bed method. Moreover, the thinner profile means that valuable space is not wasted in an already small bathroom, for instance, and that the walls don't have to be framed out above the tiled area to make them flush. Such installations weigh less than a third as much as thick-set installations. Thin-set has become the standard form of installation; however, it cannot be used in every situation. Your installer may recommend mud-set for a floor or wall, depending upon its location, condition, and the specific tile.

## MORTARS AND ADHESIVES

Your installer will select the most appropriate mortar or adhesive for each job depending upon several factors, including the method of installation, location, function, type of tile, and budget. He or she should use only products that meet standards set by the American National Standards Institute. Options fall into two categories:

*Portland-cement mortar* is generally used with thick-set installations because it is relatively inexpensive. A mixture of portland cement and sand, it is usually used for floors; lime is added for walls. Specialized types include:

• Dry-set mortar: A mixture of portland cement with sand and additives that retain water, eliminating the need to soak tiles.

• Latex-portland-cement mortar: Similar to dry-set mortar, but the latex additive—an emulsion of rubber or resin particles in water—replaces all or part of the water in the mortar mix. This formulation provides better adhesion, density, and impact strength than dry-set mortar and is more flexible and resistant to frost damage.

• Modified epoxy emulsion mortar: A resin and a hardener are blended with portland cement and sand. More economical than epoxy mortar, not as chemical-resistant, but forms a better bond, and compared to plain portland-cement mortar results in minimal shrinkage.

*Thin-set adhesives* are designed to be strong in a relatively thin application. Despite their name, they also can be used in thick-set jobs, although such use is expensive. Varieties include:

• Epoxy mortar: A two- or three-part mortar (resin and hardener with silica filler) that has high chemical resistance, strong bonding quality, and high resistance to impact.

• Epoxy adhesive: Similar to epoxy mortar but not as chemical- or solvent-resistant.

• Organic adhesive: A one-part mastic that requires no mixing and is more economical than epoxy mortar or adhesive. Compared to portland cement, it remains somewhat flexible. Has good bonding quality but should not be used for exterior or constantly wet areas.

• Furan mortar: A two-part mortar (furan resin and hardener) used in commercial applications where high heat and chemical tolerance is necessary.

## FINALLY, THE GROUT

Once the tile has set and any sealer has dried, the installer forces grout into the spaces between the tiles with a rubber float or a squeegee, working one small area at a time. Excess grout is carefully removed by wiping the float across the tile

## Maintaining Grout

Berries and wine can stain grout, and vinegar, lemon juice, and other acids can bleach or discolor cementitious grout. To remove grease and stains, use a neutral-Ph detergent cleanser. For more stubborn stains, follow the manufacturer's recommendations, which may advise using a 20-percent-strength mix of phosphoric acid (available at hardware stores) and water. Be sure to carefully follow all instructions on the cleanser's label.

at a 90-degree angle to the surface and then wiping the tiles clean. In certain instances, the grout must damp-cure, which means keeping it moist for up to 36 hours. Floors should not be walked on for at least 1 day and sometimes 3 or 4 days following installation; use plywood boards over kraft paper if it is absolutely necessary to cross the area.

When it comes to choosing grout, there is a wide range of options. Grout once had a bad rap because of its tendency to crack and stain. Today numerous formulations have been developed for specific uses, making it more flexible, water-resistant, stainproof, and mildew-resistant. Latex additives in the form of a milky liquid or a powder add flexibility and water resistance, and enable any dye in the grout to be distributed more uniformly. Assuming a sound base, proper installation, and good care, grout should perform well for decades. Some tiles can be stained by grout. If you are using a dark color grout, do a test to make sure it doesn't get caught in small depressions or hairline cracks. You may want to use a grout release product before grouting to make removal from the tiles easier.

The roughly eight varieties of grout fall into three basic categories: those with a portland-cement base; others with an epoxy, furan, or silicone base; and the newest kind, polymers. The two most important issues in deciding what grout to use are joint width and stain resistance; chemical resistance can also be a factor. Your tile installer or retailer will recommend a grout based on the type of tile, its location, the underlayment, and any special factors, such as dampness or freezing conditions.

Portland-cement grout has a relatively rough appearance due to its sand content, and is used when grout lines are more than ⅛ inch wide. It looks particularly good with rustic handmade tiles where it can compensate for irregularities in size. When used in thick-set installations, the grout may require damp curing, during which the installation must be kept wet for several days. Relatively porous, some cement grouts can be sealed with silicone or penetrating sealers. Latex-portland-cement grout has additives that make it more water-resistant and flexible and minimize the need for damp curing. Note: Cementitious grout must be wiped off irregular surfaces, such as faux stone ceramic tiles, before it dries, or it may prove impossible to remove.

Epoxy-based grouts are formulated to resist chemicals, stains, mold, and mildew, and are impervious to water, making them ideal for use on countertops. They are also more appropriate for thinner joints. White epoxy grouts, which yellow with exposure to ultraviolet light and need special cleansers, can be difficult to install and more expensive than other grouts. However, they are also the most colorfast and can resist acidic foods that may discolor and damage cement grout. Most require mixing of two or three components. Note: Epoxy grout must be removed from tiles before it hardens.

Self-sealing, stain-resistant polymer grouts, a recent development, come premixed in an array of colors.

Sealers must be applied carefully to cement-based grout to block stains and smooth the surface. Silicone-based sealers, which penetrate the joint, are suitable for areas exposed to water; acrylics are fine for other surfaces. Neither should be applied until the grout has completely cured (28 days after installation). Sealers must be applied carefully to ensure that all seams are filled and will need to be reapplied. Overzealous scrubbing with a brush will take off the sealer. Grout color may need to be touched up with a grout stain after sealer is applied.

## SEAL FOR SATISFACTION

Some unglazed tile develops a natural soft patina as it ages, an appealing look where water and stains are not a problem. But terra cotta must be sealed to be water- and stain-resistant, a necessity in kitchens, baths, and other rooms where spills are likely. (Some terra cotta is sold already sealed, or pretreated; others are sold unsealed, or raw.) Unglazed and encaustic tiles also often need sealing for use in certain areas.

Sealers fall into two general categories—penetrating and surface—and either can be water- or solvent-based. Some penetrating sealers do not change the look of the tile, others darken the tile slightly, and still others give the tile a distinct "wet look." Surface sealers, which are usually formulated from acrylic or urethane, impart a higher gloss, highlighting the natural character and color of the tile. In most cases, sealer is applied after the tile is laid but before it is grouted. Your installer or retailer will recommend a specific sealer depending upon three factors: the porosity of the tile, where it is to be installed, and the look desired. Generally a water-based product will serve in a bathroom or hallway, where moisture resistance is key; a solvent-based one is usually better where grease is the culprit. All sealers have to be reapplied as they wear down; penetrating types merely need a new coat, but surface sealers must be removed every few years before reapplication.

After on-site sealing and grouting, terra cotta can then be waxed with a compatible product to give either a shiny or matte look; tinted wax can further darken tiles. Alternatively, boiled linseed oil in combination with mineral spirits, followed by wax, will intensify the natural color of terra cotta (and quarry tile). Many professionals swear by this relatively  inexpensive method, but it is not always an effective stain protector, is flammable, and releases volatile organic compounds into the atmosphere. Traditionally, the French apply beeswax over raw terra cotta, a method that fills in tiny holes and over time develops a leatherlike patina. Once sealed, terra cotta can be maintained with regular sweeping and an occasional damp mopping. Avoid sealing terra cotta with polyurethane. Not only does it give the floor a yellow cast, but because it sits on top of the tile, any moisture that works its way in through tiny scratches will cause an unattractive milky look.

You may want to seal quarry tile for a "wet" look or to enhance stain resistance in kitchens. If you clean the floor regularly with an oil-based liquid household cleaner, it will become seasoned and develop a patina with age. However, if the floor will be subject to greasy spills, you may want to use a manufacturer-recommended product to seal the floor before it is grouted. An alternative sealing method (after the floor has been grouted and the grout has cured) is to apply

Murphy's Oil Soap or another oil-based cleaner full-strength and let it sit for 30 minutes. Then remove any excess liquid with a clean dry rag. Finally, wash the floor, following the procedure recommended on the cleaner's label. Repeat the process the next day and periodically until the floor develops a patina. For a higher luster, use a mop on a clean floor to apply a surface acrylic sealer such as Mop & Glo or a product made by the tile manufacturer. Apply several thin coats, stroking in one direction, then another, to avoid streaks. For a lower sheen, dilute the sealer with an equal amount of water. Check the manufacturer's recommendations before applying any sealer.

## ONGOING MAINTENANCE

Generally, tile needs to be washed less frequently than other surfaces that receive the same amount of soil and use. Treat your ceramic floor well and it will reward you with decades of service. Follow manufacturer's recommendations and give special care to floors and bathroom walls, which each have a few special requirements.

### IMMEDIATELY AFTER INSTALLATION

The best way to treat your newly tiled surface is to stay off it as long as possible. The more time the grout is given to cure, the stronger, denser, and more water-resistant it becomes. After allowing the grout to dry for at least 24 and preferably 48 hours, wipe any dirt or markings off the tile with a sponge or a sponge mop and plain water. If there are remaining yellow or clear marks, use a soft-scrub cleaning product on a bristle brush, then rinse thoroughly. If the tile has a whitish haze from a residue of drying grout, gently wipe it off with a damp sponge. Be careful not to disturb the freshly grouted joint lines. If a second hazing occurs, polish with a soft clean cloth. For truly stubborn mortar deposits on unglazed tiles, a mild solution of white vinegar or sulfamic acid crystals (available at hardware stores) and water can be wiped on and then rinsed thoroughly. Do not apply the diluted acid solution in direct sunlight and never use muriatic acid for any purpose.

## INSIDE JOBS

Vacuum, dry-mop, or sweep floors frequently—daily if possible—to remove grains of dirt that can scratch tiled surfaces; damp-wipe or sponge-mop occasionally. Work on a small area at a time, wringing out the sponge and changing the water often. Wipe up spills immediately; if a residue remains, spritz with a window-cleaning product. All-purpose soapless detergents mixed with hot water will handle heavy soil. Using a sponge mop, apply the cleaning solution to a small area and leave it for about a minute to loosen the dirt before scrubbing with the mop. Use a nylon scrubbing pad for hard-to-remove marks. Repeat this process until the whole floor has been washed, then rinse thoroughly with clean warm water, wringing frequently. With the exception of waxed terra cotta, ceramic tile does not require buffing or polishing. Give kitchen counters the same treatment using a sponge or rag instead of a sponge mop.

If you have treated your tiles with a surface sealer, periodically you should remove the sealer with hot water and ammonia and apply a new coat.

The enemies of shower and bath walls are deposits from hard water, soap scum, and body oils. Again, the best approach is to prevent buildup with regular cleaning. Use a detergent-based cleanser, since soap builds up a scum that holds dirt, promotes the growth of mildew and bacteria, and dulls ceramic tile's shine. It can also make the tile surface dangerously slippery when wet. For really stubborn stains, allow the detergent to sit on the tile for several minutes, then scrub with a nylon pad or scrub brush. (Test an inconspicuous area of metallic-glazed or high-gloss tiles before proceeding.) Be sure to rinse off household cleaners thoroughly as they can stain white grout.

To avoid mildew in bathrooms, install a fan and run it for several minutes after you bathe or shower, and leave the door or shower curtain open when not in use. Also use mildew-resistant grout. Mildew can be controlled with the use of XR-14, a product found in tile stores. Never mix bleach with ammonia or household cleaners that contain ammonia and never use bleach on colored grout. Hard-water deposits can be removed with a mild solution of white vinegar and water.

## OUTDOOR CHORES

Exterior walls of ceramic tile rarely need cleaning. If desired, use warm water and detergent. Wash with a soft bristle brush and rinse with clear water. Patios and paths can be hosed down routinely; clean dirt and stains as in interior situations.

Efflorescence is crystalline deposit that sometimes appears as a whitish powder or crust on the surface of grout lines or tiles. This is caused by the reaction of moisture with impurities in mortar and is thus more common in exterior installations or where a cement mortar base was used. While most likely to occur soon after installation, it can recur at any time.

The best way to eliminate the problem is to remove the source of the moisture. If this is not possible, use a stiff bristle brush, either dry or with clean water, and rinse thoroughly. As a last resort on unglazed tile only, you can use a sulfamic acid solution. For white or gray grout use a 5 to 10 percent solution; for colored grout use 2 percent. Soak the surface with water, then wash on the acid solution, scrub with a nylon bristle brush, and immediately flush with clear water. Warning: If the surface is not completely rinsed, an off-white deposit may remain that is even more difficult to remove than the original marks. Be sure to test a sulfamic acid solution in an inconspicuous area before proceeding.

## POOL UPKEEP

Tile actually makes it easier to keep a pool looking clean. With a concrete surface, tile is practically a necessity. Without it, you end up with a bathtub ring effect where dirt, body oils, and water deposits build up scum, an unattractive look that is actually magnified by the water. (Algae and dust that accumulate beneath the water's surface are removed with regular vacuuming.) Maintaining the smooth surface of a tile border, in contrast, is relatively easy. Simply use a nylon scrub pad and some elbow grease. For more stubborn stains and calcium deposits from hard water, the National Spa and Pool Institute suggests using an acid-based cleaning product recommended by the tile manufacturer or pool installer.

# Glossary

**Abrasion resistance** A measure of a tile's ability to withstand wear by friction.

**Azulejos** Portuguese or Spanish glazed blue-and-white wall tiles.

**Backer board** Water-resistant board used underneath a thin-set installation. Also known as cementitious backer board.

**Backsplash** The area above a counter or between the top of the base cabinet or counter and the base of the upper unit; also called a splashback.

**Bicottura** Italian term that refers to the method of firing a tile once to produce a bisque, then glazing and refiring it to fix decoration.

**Bisque** Tile that has been fired once, but not glazed. Also known as biscuit or bisquit; also refers to fired tile underneath a glaze.

**Bullnose** A trim tile with a convex rounded edge to finish outside corners.

**Button back** Small buttonlike protuberances on the underside of a tile that facilitate airflow in the kiln.

**Ceramic** Fired clay or a mixture of clay and other inorganic material, either glazed or unglazed.

**Ceramic mosaics** Tiles with facial area of less than 6 square inches.

**Chemical resistance** The ability of a tile to resist stains or damage from household cleaners, acids, and alkalis.

**Clay** A mixture of kaolin (aluminum silicate), quartz (sand), and traces of minerals such as iron and feldspar, which is plastic when wet.

**Cove** A concave curved molding that bridges an inside corner or where a vertical and a horizontal surface meet.

**Crazing** Fine hairline cracking on a glaze that can indicate age or stress. When used intentionally to create an aged effect, a crazed glaze will be indicated by the manufacturer.

**Culinarios** Portuguese glazed wall tiles that depict polychrome fruit and vegetables, traditionally used in kitchens.

**Curing** Process during which a new tile installation sets.

**Deck** The horizontal surface around a bathtub.

**Delftware** Tin-glazed earthenware, originally made in Holland, covered with an opaque white glaze and blue, magenta, or polychrome decoration.

**Dust-pressed** Tiles formed by compressing clay dust mixed with a small amount of moisture under great weight.

**Eased** Natural or sloped edges rather than sharp, ground edges; also known as relieved.

**Efflorescence** Residue on surface of tile or grout joint formed by the crystallization of soluble salts.

**Encaustic** A tile with a design made by inlaying one or more differently colored clays in the clay body.

**Expansion joint** A joint filled with flexible material, which can expand or contract slightly without cracking the surrounding tile.

**Extruded** Tile formed from malleable, plastic clay forced through a die, wire-cut, and fired, resulting in sharp, flat edges.

**Flashing** Natural marks resulting from the chemical reaction of oxides in clay during the firing process.

**Frit** Ground-up glass and other ceramic materials that form the medium of a glaze and carry the pigments.

**Frost-resistant** Suitable for outside installation in climates subject to extremes of temperature.

**Gauge** Thickness of tile.

**Glaze** A glass compound colored with metal oxide that bonds chemically to the clay or bisque when fired.

**Ground** Edges that have been cut to form a sharp 90-degree angle; in contrast to relieved or eased edges.

**Grout** Material used to fill in the spaces between tiles.

**Impervious** Tiles that have minimal porosity (0.5 percent or less).

**Inserts** Small, sometimes decorative tiles used in combination with larger, plain tiles to create patterns; also known as keystones, keys, or dots.

**Kiln** An oven for the controlled firing of tile.

**Liner** A narrow, usually flat tile used to add interest to field tiles; also known as a *listello* in Italy.

**Luster** Metallic or iridescent glaze resulting from the addition of copper, silver, gold, or bronze powders.

**Majolica** A yellow-pink bisque, relatively porous, usually refired with a nontransparent glaze and used for interior walls.

**Mastic** An adhesive compound used for installing tile.

**Mechanical strength** A measurement used for floor tiles that reflects strength and resistance to breaking when flexed.

**Membrane** A layer of sheeting that separates the backing surface from tile mortar to protect from water, cracks, or other instability; also known as a cleavage membrane.

**Mitred** Cut on an angle to meet complementary cut tile on either an edge or a corner.

**Monocottura** Italian term meaning a single-step firing in which the clay body (bisque) and glazing processes take place simultaneously.

**Mortar** Tile-setting medium used to bond tiles to a surface.

**Mosaic** Small pieces of tile, glass, or stone laid to create a pattern. Also the industry term for tiles with a facial area of less than 6 square inches.

**Mud-set** Installation method in which tile is laid in a cement base of ¾ to 2 inches.

**Nonvitreous** Tiles that have a porosity of more than 7 percent.

**Paver** A floor tile of more than 6 square inches formed by the dust-pressed method, usually with an eased, relieved, or "natural" edge when viewed in profile.

**Pillowed** With a slightly rounded profile, like a flattened pillow.

**Pique assiette** A French word that translates literally as "broken plate" but refers to a mosaic of broken tile; also known as rubble.

**Porcelain** A dense, impervious, fine-grained and smooth tile with a sharply formed face made by the dust-pressed method.

**Porosity** The property that determines the amount of water that the unglazed portion of the tile absorbs.

**Provençal** Curvaceous shaped tile such as an ogee typical of Spanish and Moorish design.

**Quarry tile** A natural clay floor tile, generally at least ½ inch thick, produced by extrusion; can be glazed or unglazed.

**Relieved** See Eased.

**Riser** The vertical part of a stair.

**Rubble** Broken tile pieces used to create a mosaic.

**Saltillo** A Mexican tile made of unprocessed clay from a certain region.

**Sealer** A coating that protects unglazed tile and grout from moisture and stains or adds luster.

**Semivitreous** Tiles with more than 3 percent and less than 7 percent porosity.

**Slip-resistant** The property of floor tiles that should be considered in wet areas,

outdoors, or indoors immediately adjoining outdoor areas, resulting from abrasive materials mixed into the clay or applied to the surface, grooves, or patterns in the surface, or a glaze specifically designed for an increased coefficient of friction.

**Spacers** Small plastic pieces used to maintain even joints between tiles.

**Special-purpose tile** Tile made to have special physical or appearance characteristics. Most handcrafted tile falls into this category, as does slip-resistant

tile and those resistant to staining or frost or fabricated for other special conditions.

**Surround** The walls encircling a bathtub or shower area.

**Terra cotta** Fired raw earth; used primarily for floor tile; sometimes is glazed.

**Thick-bed** See Mud-set.

**Thin-set** Installation method that uses a bond-coating of less than ¾ inch applied to a flat surface.

**Toe space** Area at the base of cabinets that is inset to accommodate feet; also called toe kick and kickplate.

**Vitreous** Tiles that have a porosity of more than 0.5 percent but less than 3 percent; also known as vitrified.

**Water absorption** See Porosity.

**Zellij** Traditional Moroccan hand-cut, glazed tiles.

# Further Reading and Information

The following books and videos will provide information on the history of tile, tile design, and installation techniques. Many can be ordered through the Tile Heritage Foundation (see Directory of Resources, page 195).

## HISTORY OF TILE

Barnard, Julian. *Victorian Ceramic Tiles,* Studio Vista Publishers, London, 1972.

Beaulah, Kenneth. *Church Tiles of the Nineteenth Century,* Shire Publications, Ltd., Aylesbury, Great Britain, 1987.

Catleugh, Jon. *William DeMorgan Tiles,*

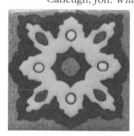

Richard Dennis Publications, Somerset, Great Britain, 1991.

Chipman, Jack. *The Collector's Encyclopedia of California Pottery,* Collector Books, Paducah, KY, 1991.

Lockett, Terence A. *Collecting Victorian Tiles,* Baron Publications, New York, 1988.

Herbert, Tony, and Kathryn Huggins. *The Decorative Tile in Architecture and Interiors,* Phaidon Press, London, 1995.

Reed, Cleota. *Henry Chapman Mercer & The Moravian Pottery & Tile Works,* University of Pennsylvania Press, Philadelphia, 1987.

Riley, Noel. *Tile Art: A History of Decorative Ceramic Tiles,* Magna Books, Leichester, Great Britain, 1992.

Rindge, Ronald L. *Ceramic Art of Malibu Potteries,* Malibu-Laguna Museum Press, Malibu, CA, 1988.

Rosenthal, Lee. *Catalina Tile of the Magic Isle,* Windgate Press, Sausalito, CA, 1992.

Van Lemmen, Hans. *Decorative Tiles Throughout the Ages,* Crescent Books, London, 1988.

———. *Delftware Tiles,* Shire Publications, Ltd., Aylesbury, Great Britain, 1986.

———. *Tiles: A Collector's Guide,* Souvenir Press, London, 1979.

———. *Tiles: 1,000 Years of Architectural Decoration,* Harry N. Abrams, Inc., New York, 1993.

———. *Tiled Furniture,* Shire Publications, Ltd., Aylesbury, Great Britain, 1989.

Van Lemmen, Hans, and John Malam, eds. *Fired Earth: 1000 Years of Tiles in Europe,* Richard Dennis Publications, Somerset, Great Britain, 1991.

## TILE DESIGN

Coyle, Carolyn. *Designing with Tile,* Van Nostrand Reinhold, New York, 1994.

Giorgini, Frank. *Handmade Tiles,* Lark Books, Asheville, NC, 1994.

Grafton, Carol Belanger. *Decorative Tile Design,* Dover Press, New York, 1987.

———. *Decorative Tile Designs in Full Color,* Dover Press, New York, 1992.

Hilliard, Elizabeth. *Designing with Tiles,* Abbeville Press, New York, 1993.

King, Carol Soucek. *Designing with Tile, Stone & Brick,* PBC International, Glen Cove, NY, 1995.

Siegel, Roslyn, with Norman Karlson. *Country Floor's Decorating with Tiles,* Simon & Schuster, New York, 1989.

## INSTALLING TILE

Burch, Monte. *Tile Indoors & Out,* Creative Homeowner Press, Passaic, NJ, 1981.

Byrne, Michael. *Setting Ceramic Tile,* Taunton Press, Newtown, CT, 1987.

Kerrigone, Kimberly, ed. *Working with Tile,* Creative Homeowner Press, Passaic, NJ, 1993.

Ortho Books Editors and Jill Fox. *How to Install Ceramic Tile,* Karin Shakery, ed., Ortho Books, 1989.

Ramsey, Dan. *Tile Floors: Installing, Maintaining and Repairing,* Tab Books, Blue Ridge Summit, PA, 1985.

Southern Living Staff, ed. *Tile Remodeling Handbook,* Oxmoor House, Birmingham, AL, 1992.

Sunset Magazine and Book Editors. *Ceramic Tile,* Sunset Publications, Menlo Park, CA, 1987.

## CULTURAL INSPIRATION

Binney, Marcus. *Country Manors of Portugal,* Scala Books, Harper & Row, New York, 1987.

Dennis, Landt. *Morocco: Design from Casablanca to Marrakesh,* Clarkson N. Potter, Inc., New York, 1992.

Slesin, Suzanne, et al. *Spanish Style,* Clarkson N. Potter, Inc., New York, 1990.

## HOW-TO VIDEOS

*Ceramic Tile, Planning and Installation,* Hometime Video Publishing, Chaska, MS, 1994.

*Tiling Countertops with Michael Byrne,* A Fine Homebuilding Video Workshop, Taunton Books & Videos, Newtown, CT, 1987.

*Tiling Floors with Michael Byrne,* A Fine Homebuilding Video Workshop, Taunton Books & Videos, Newtown, CT, 1987.

*Tiling Walls with Michael Bryne,* A Fine Homebuilding Video Workshop, Taunton Books & Videos, Newtown, CT, 1987.

# Directory of Resources

It would take a vast volume to list all the manufacturers and vendors of tile; space demands that we list just a few of the many suppliers. Shops that sell nothing but tile (and often stone) have sprung up in major cities and suburban areas across the country. Where once Country Floors was virtually the sole purveyor of handcrafted tiles, companies such as Ann Sacks Tile & Stone, Waterworks, and Walker Zanger now have multiple showrooms. Most large cities also have local retailers with large selections, as well as custom studios that sell directly. Some manufacturers, such as Summitville, Dal-Tile, and American Olean, have retail stores nationwide. Some vendors, however, sell only to the trade; you will have to work with an architect or designer to purchase from them. TileNet, a service of the Tile Promotion Board, links up consumers with local tile dealers who subscribe to the service. Call 800-495-5900 for more information.

## NATIONAL SPECIALTY SHOWROOMS

These tile retailers (most are importers and wholesalers as well) have several showrooms, as listed. They also sell their products through distributors. All will help buyers work out the intricacies of a design and offer catalogs of their product lines.

### ANN SACKS TILE & STONE

500 NW 23rd Avenue
Portland, OR 97210
503-331-7320 (Western states)
212-463-0492 (Eastern states)
Extraordinary selection of handcrafted and factory-made ceramic tile, antique tile, and stone from the United States and abroad. Showrooms in New York City, Seattle, Portland, San Francisco, Los Angeles, Chicago, Kohler, WI, and Vancouver, B.C. 160-page catalog: $16.

### COUNTRY FLOORS

8735 Melrose Avenue
West Hollywood, CA 90069
310-657-0510
Specializes in painted wares from France, Spain, Portugal, Holland, as well as antique and new terra-cotta and other ceramic and stone tiles of every description. Showrooms in New York City, Los Angeles, Miami, Philadelphia, and San Francisco; representatives in most major cities. Catalog of imported tiles: $15; domestic tiles: $10.

### ELON, INC.

5 Skyline Drive
Elmsford, NY 10523
914-347-7744
Traditional, imported, handcrafted, or hand-painted wall tiles and handmade terra-cotta floor tiles, plus reclaimed terra cotta; 78-page catalog: $10. Also American hand-painted line; 24-page catalog: $4. Showrooms in Los Angeles, New York City, Chicago, San Antonio, Miami, and Elmsford, NY; represented by many other dealers.

### PARIS CERAMICS

31 East Elm Street
Greenwich, CT 06830
203-862-9538
Hand-painted, handmade, unique tiles produced by British artists and antique terra cotta salvaged from old French buildings; also custom work. Showrooms in New York City, Los Angeles, Greenwich, CT, and London. Free catalog.

### WALKER ZANGER WEST COAST

8901 Bradley Avenue
Sun Valley, CA 91352
818-504-0235
Painted and molded tiles, both domestic and imported. Showrooms in Los Angeles, Costa Mesa, and Sun Valley, CA, Honolulu, and Houston. Sold nationwide by more than 150 distributors. 80-page catalog: $12; custom ideas booklet: $4.

### WATERWORKS

29 Park Avenue
Danbury, CT 06810
800-89WORKS
American handcrafted tile; also European bathroom fixtures and fittings. Showrooms in Westport, Danbury, and Greenwich, CT, New York City, Boston, Dallas, San Francisco, Los Angeles, and Chicago. Catalog: $10.

## OTHER SPECIALTY SHOWROOMS

Most will assist with design and recommend installers. The larger the inventory, usually the faster the delivery.

### New York and Tristate Area

#### CERAMICA ARNON, INC.

134 West 20th Street
New York, NY 10011
212-807-0876
Israeli-born Arnon Zadok is a third-generation master tile setter, who also sells unique and handmade domestic and imported products.

### DESIGN SUPPLY
215 Park Avenue South
New York, NY 10003
212-979-6400
Fine production and hard-molded lines,
including Pewabic, Motawi, Tricanen,
FireClay, as well as Victorian transfer reproductions and other unusual items. Primarily to
the trade.

### HASTINGS TILE & IL BAGNO
230 Park Avenue South
New York, NY 10003
212-674-9700
Comprehensive source of high-end tiles and
bath furnishings, including Italian cutting-edge
design. Showrooms also in Great Neck and
Huntington, NY, Chicago Design Mart, and
distributors nationwide.

### NEMO TILE COMPANY
48 East 21st Street
New York, NY 10010
212-505-0009
Large importer, selling tile from Italy, Spain,
Portugal, France, and Brazil, plus major
American manufacturers.

### TILES: A REFINED SELECTION
42 West 15th Street
New York, NY 10011
212-255-4450
Huge selection of handmade and otherwise
special tiles.

### WESTPORT TILE & DESIGN
175 Post Road West
Westport, CT 06880
203-454-0032
Extensive collection of ceramic tile and natural
stone; also represents Ann Sacks and Hastings.

## New England
### BOSTON TILE
25 McNeil Way
Dedham, MA 02026
617-461-0406
Factory-made tile from Italy and Spain; also
domestic brands like U.S. Ceramic and
Tileworks. Stores throughout East Coast.

### SHEP BROWN ASSOCIATES, INC.
24 Cummings Park
Woburn, MA 01801
617-935-8080
Exclusive line of imported artisan and factory-
made tiles; serving professionals and homeowners.

### TILE SHOWCASE
291 Arsenal Street
Watertown, MA 02172
617-926-1100
Enormous selection of imported and domestic,
factory-made and handmade tile, including
Hastings, Country Floors, Candy Tile's English
reproductions of William Morris and William
De Morgan designs, and Victorian transferware. Showroom also in Southboro.

### TILES: A REFINED SELECTION
115 Newbury Street
Boston, MA 02116
617-437-0400
Huge selection of handmade tiles; parent of
the New York City store of the same name.

## Florida & Southeast
### FORMS & SURFACES
3801 NE Second Avenue
Miami, FL 33137
305-576-1880
Specializes in stone, imported floor tile, and
solid-color wall tile.

### IBERIA TILES
2975 NW 77 Avenue
Miami, FL 33122
305-591-3880
Huge retailer of Spanish, Italian, and South
American tile, plus Laufen International,
American Marazzi, and other domestic tiles;
showrooms also in Pompano Beach and Coral
Gables.

### RENAISSANCE TILE & BATH
349 Peachtree Hills Avenue, NE
Atlanta, GA 30305
404-231-9203
Unusual tile from small artisans like Talisman,
Fire & Earth, and California Potteries;
represents Hastings and Country Floors.

### SUNNY MCLEAN & COMPANY
3800 NE Second Avenue
Miami, FL 33137
305-573-5943
Enormous selection of unique, handmade and
imported tile, stone, and cement products.

## Northern California
### BEDROSIAN TILE & MARBLE
426 Littlefield Avenue
South San Francisco, CA 94080
415-876-0100
Factory-made Italian, Spanish, and Japanese
products and domestic tile from American
Marazzi, Monarch, and Metropolitan
Ceramics. Showrooms in California, Nevada,
Arizona, Colorado, and Utah.

### CARMEL TILE & MARBLE
26382 Carmel Ranch Lane
Carmel, CA 93923
408-625-6216
Broad selection of unusual handcrafted tiles,
including regional crafts.

### NISSAN TILE & MARBLE
364 Bayshore Boulevard
San Francisco, CA 94124
415-641-4500
Italian and other imported factory-made tile as
well as products by American Olean, Florida
Tile, and Mannington.

### TILECRAFT
135 Rhode Island Street
San Francisco, CA 94103
415-552-1913
Handcrafted and imported tile, including
Walker Zanger. Branches also in San Jose, San
Rafael, and Walnut Creek.

## Southern California
### BOLIVAR, INC.
1 West California Boulevard
Suite 111
Pasadena, CA 91105
818-449-8453
Sylvie Atanasio carries tile and ceramic acces-
sories from small American artisans, plus a few
Italian, Portuguese, and Mexican lines.

**BRIAN FLYNN TILES**
Pacific Design Center B447
8687 Melrose Drive
Los Angeles, CA 90069
310-659-2614
Trendsetters Brian Flynn and Susi Parker represent leading tile artists. To the trade only; also distribute to retailers as California Art Tile (800-646-8453).

**CONCEPT STUDIO**
2720 East Coast Highway
Corona del Mar, CA 92625
714-759-0606
Richard Goddard and Karen Bishop produce their own lines of fine handmade tile and sell other artisans' work; their line is distributed nationally.

**FROM THE GROUND UP**
7760 Fay Avenue
La Jolla, CA 92037
619-551-9902
Diane Koehnick sells handcrafted tile, primarily American made.

**MISSION TILE WEST**
853 Mission Street
South Pasadena, CA 91030
818-799-4595
Thano Adamson handles Alchemie Ceramic, Native Tile, Motawi, and other artisans as well as factory-made imports and domestic tiles.

**NS CERAMIC**
401 East Carrillo
Santa Barbara, CA 93101
805-962-1422
Nola Stucky offers American art tiles, imported Tunisian ceramics, and other unusual items; specializes in historical renovations.

**SOUTHWESTERN CERAMIC TILE**
5525 Gaines Street
San Diego, CA 92110
619-298-3511
Italian, Brazilian, Spanish, and Portuguese imports as well as American Olean and American Marazzi tile; a Walker Zanger distributor.

**THE STUDIO**
1925 State Street
Santa Barbara, CA 93101
805-563-2003
Douglas and Marjorie Gheza design and sell handmade tile, including the Country Floors line.

### Mountain Region

**CAPCO, INC.**
5101 East Evans Avenue
Denver, CO 80222
303-759-1919
Wholesaler importing from Italy, Spain, Portugal, Japan, Korea, Thailand, Venezuela, and Brazil. Showroom open to the public; will recommend local dealers.

**EUROBATH & TILE**
1923 Market Street
Denver, CO 80202
303-298-8453
Custom tile imported by Walker Zanger, Hastings, and others, much of it handmade. To the trade only.

**IBERIA TILE**
1939 Blake Street
Denver, CO 80223
303-298-1883
Italian and Spanish factory-made tiles plus handmade American works by Ken Mason, Deer Creek, Stellar, and Moore-Merkowitz; also represents Country Floors; two locations.

### Southwest

**ARIZONA TILE**
550 East Thomas Road
Phoenix, AZ 85018
602-279-4478
Outlets also in Tucson, Scottsdale, Tempe, Prescott, and Glendale; carries tile from major American manufacturers such as Summitville.

**CERAMICA**
3039 East Main Street
Scottsdale, AZ 85251
602-990-7074
Imports from Italy, Spain, Portugal, India, China, Turkey, and Greece; domestic tile from Stellar, Deer Creek, Surving, and other small studios; represents Walker Zanger, Hastings, and Epstone.

**CONWAY TILE**
5401 East 29th Street
Tucson, AZ 85711
520-747-9636
Primarily domestic factory-made tile from Monarch, Dal-Tile, and American Olean, plus Arizona Tile and some imports.

**COUNTERPOINT TILES**
1519 Paseo de Peralta
Santa Fe, NM 87501
505-982-1247
Connie and Ronda Kay make their own tiles and sell products by other artisans from New Mexico and around the country. Brochure: $3.

**FACINGS OF AMERICA**
4121 North 27th Street
Phoenix, AZ 85016
602-955-9217
Innovative showroom with large line of factory-made imports from Italy and Spain, plus American factories like McIntyre, Stellar, and Latco; a Walker Zanger distributor.

**STATEMENTS IN TILE**
1441 Paseo de Peralta
Santa Fe, NM 87501
505-988-4440
Interesting Mexican and French floor tiles, primarily machine-made, and solid-color Mexican Talavera-style tiles. Will ship anywhere.

### Texas

**AMERICAN TILE SUPPLY, INC.**
2839 Merrell Road
Dallas, TX 75229
214-243-2377
Huge company representing over 40 factory lines, including Laufen, Summitville, Monarch, Crossville, Florida Brick & Clay, Lone Star, plus imports. Outlets in most Texas cities.

**ANTIQUE FLOORS**
1444 Oak Lawn, Suite 850
Oak Lawn Design Plaza
Dallas, TX 75205
214-760-9330
Antique terra cotta and stone, painted tumbled marble, and ceramic mosaics, plus Walker Zanger line. To the trade only.

## HUTCHERSON TILE CO., INC.
130 Mitchell Road
Houston, TX 77037
713-447-6354
Imports from Italy, Spain, South America, Mexico, Taiwan; also domestic products. Call for retailers in Louisiana, New Mexico, Oklahoma, Mississippi, Arkansas, and Texas.

## INTILE DESIGNS
9716 Old Katy Road, Suite 110
Houston, TX 77055
713-468-4067
Factory-made tile from Italy, Spain, Mexico, Japan, Taiwan, Venezuela; 20 outlets in California, Arizona, Florida, Georgia, Texas.

## MATERIALS MARKETING CORP.
120 West Josephine
San Antonio, TX 78212
210-731-8453
Mexican and other terra-cotta tile; retail outlets also in Houston, Austin, San Diego, Chicago, and Marietta, GA; Walker Zanger and Country Floors lines in some stores. Priced brochure available.

## A UNIQUE TILE COLLECTION
2700 Carson Street
Fort Worth, TX 76117
817-831-1681
A Walker Zanger distributor.

## *Midwest*
### THE FINE LINE
209 West Illinois Street
Chicago, IL 60610
312-670-0300
Kim Preis and Kathy Kyern specialize in American tile by 30 craftsmen and small manufacturers; also represent local artisans.

## HISPANIC DESIGNÈ
6125 North Cicero
Chicago, IL 60646
312-725-3100
Imported decorative tile, including Stovax English transfer Victorian reproductions and encaustic-look tiles; Country Floors distributor; also domestic custom tile.

## INTERNATIONAL MATERIALS OF DESIGN
4585 Indian Creek Parkway
Overland, KS 66207
913-383-3383
Sarah Hines represents small American craft lines like Talisman, Epro, McIntyre, Pratt & Larsen, and Moore-Merkowitz; also imports from Country Floors and Epstone.

## MATERIALS MARKETING CORP.
357 West Chicago
Chicago, IL 60610
312-440-9666
Terra cotta and Walker Zanger line. Another showroom in Highland Park.

## *Pacific Northwest*
### PRATT & LARSEN TILE
207 Second Avenue South
Seattle, WA 98104
206-343-7907
Michael Pratt and Reta Larsen create new designs in a Craftsman spirit, reflecting such Northwest imagery as pinecones and bears. Also represent other regional tile makers at retail stores in Portland and Seattle. Line sold at all Country Floors stores. Catalog available.

## WILEY'S TILE
Seattle Design Center
5701 Sixth Avenue, Suite 127
Seattle, WA 98108
206-767-6502
To-the-trade showroom open to the public in the afternoon; orders should go through design professionals; stock includes Elon imports and handcrafted American tile by FireClay, Ken Mason, Firebird, and ME Tile.

## HANDCRAFTED TILE STUDIOS
These individuals or small companies produce distinctive handcrafted tiles. They are only a few of the hundreds of talented craftspeople at work today. Some offer literature. Most sell through one or more dealers; call for information.

## ALCHEMIE CERAMIC STUDIO
1550 Gascony Road
Leucadia, CA 92024
Laird Plumleigh's handmade high-relief tiles feature superb variegated glazes in the Craftsman tradition. Dealers include Ceramica in Scottsdale, Mission Tile in Pasadena, and Walker Zanger stores, or write for the name of a retailer near you.

## À MANO
PO Box B
Camp Meeker, CA 95419
707-874-2538
Dale Wiley makes hand-carved and press-molded tiles inspired by nature, history, and cultural influences. Custom work in region or by special arrangement. Free literature.

## ARCHITECTURAL ACCENTS
5353 West Sopris Creek Road
Basalt, CO 81621
970-927-3056
Candy Resnick and Ro Mead make custom-crafted, sculptural tile murals, often in a naturalistic style, working directly with clients nationwide. Free brochure.

## BLUE SLIDE ART TILE
207 A Street, Box 927
Point Reyes, CA 94956
415-663-1640
Gordon Bryan's luminous glazes make his playful motifs of leaping fish, frogs, elephants, and more come alive. Call California Art Tile, 800-646-8453, for closest retailer.

## BRENDA BERTIN TILES
476 Chemin des Patriots North
Mount St. Hilaire, Quebec PQ
J3H3H9
514-536-0056
Handmade tiles with glazes made from old formulas using classic ingredients like cobalt, copper, tin, and iron, some with relief motifs.

## BUSBY GILBERT TILE CO./ MALIBU GROUP
16021 Arminta Street
Van Nuys, CA 91406
818-780-9460
High-fired Malibu, Catalina, and other hand-made looks; also sculptural ceramic sea creatures and tile reproductions of fine art.

## CLAY-BIDDLE ASSOCIATES
1887 Newfield Avenue
Stamford, CT 06903
203-322-3805
Custom hand-painted tiles, plus silk-screen tile panels depicting herbs and vegetables. Free brochure.

## VEVA CROZIER
Lukkens Color
19 Rockwood Lane
Greenwich, CT 06830
203-869-4679
Vibrant one-of-a-kind hand-painted tiles; Crozier accepts commissions nationwide.

## L. CURTIS DESIGNS
145 Hudson Street
New York, NY 10013
212-966-1720
Lynda Curtis's hand-painted and -molded tiles reflect cultural influences as diverse as Stone Age wall paintings and Mayan reliefs.

## L'ESPERANCE TILE WORKS
237 Sheridan Avenue
Albany, NY 12210
518-465-5586
Linda Ellert and Don Shore's reproduction Victorian and Craftsman tiles are sold through Waterworks (800-89WORKS). They also take direct orders for custom reproductions of Victorian encaustic tiles and will match vintage glazes to replace missing tiles.

## FIRE & EARTH CERAMICS
PO Box 1427
Boulder, CO 80306
303-442-0245
Jeff Gaines's lush tiles come in luster, raku, and crystalline glazes in 50 colors and as many shapes; also ceramic murals. Distributed through Ann Sacks and other showrooms.

## MARION GREBOW
123 Picketts Ridge Road
West Redding, CT 06896
203-938-4188
Grebow custom designs hand-painted and hand-molded relief tiles to a client's wishes.

## MICHELLE GRIFFOUL STUDIOS
PO Box 588
Los Olivos, CA 93441
805-688-9631
Griffoul designs free-form tiles in the shape of fish, leaves, flowers, and more. Represented by Ann Sacks.

## KALLEN ARCHITECTURAL CERAMICS
1431-A 34th Avenue
Seattle, WA 98122
206-720-1774
Kathryn Allen carves one-of-a-kind tiles in high-relief designs, some with raku glazes.

## MALIBU ART TILE
23852 Pacific Coast Highway
Suite 116
Malibu, CA 90265
818-706-7369; 818-706-2766
Lindell Lummer and Angelique Ferrari make hand-molded reproductions of colorful Malibu tiles. Literature upon request; full catalog: $5.

## KEN MASON TILE, INC.
809 West 15th Street
Long Beach, CA 90813
310-432-7574
Custom glazed tiles in rich colors and patterns. Distributed through Country Floors; overruns sold directly. Literature available.

## THE MEREDITH COLLECTION
PO Box 8854
Canton, OH 44711
216-484-1656
Rachel Renkert makes Arts and Crafts–style and contemporary tiles with an antique hand press; 40 different glazes. Widely distributed. Free brochure.

## MOORE-MERKOWITZ COLLECTION
5552 East Valley Road
Alfred Station, NY 14803
607-587-9508
Susan Moore and Neil Merkowitz make intricately molded tiles and moldings that evoke the English and American Arts and Crafts traditions. Available through Ann Sacks and other dealers. Catalog in the works.

## MOTAWI TILEWORKS
33 North Staebler Road
Ann Arbor, MI 48103
313-971-0765
Nawal and Karim Motawi make relief tiles in the Art Nouveau, Mission, Celtic, and Arts and Crafts traditions. Motifs include griffins, stags, rabbits, birds of paradise, and tree bark. Fireplace tile surrounds and hearths can be adapted to any space. Catalog available.

## NATIVE TILE & CERAMICS
4230 Glencoe Avenue
Marina del Rey, CA 90292
310-823-8684
Diana and Tom Watson make handcrafted decorative tile, including Mission, Craftsman, Art Deco, Batchelder, Malibu, and Catalina looks. Also a line of tiles inspired by patchwork quilts, and custom "Oriental rugs."

## SHEL NEYMARK
PO Box 25
Embudo, NM 87531
505-579-4432
High-relief, whimsical hand-painted tiles and custom murals, fireplaces, columns, and fountains; catalog: $3.

## PEACE VALLEY TILE
64 Buelah Road
New Britain, PA 18901
215-340-0888
Will Mead handmakes extruded tiles, then
hand-smoothes the edges; both unglazed and
with luminous glazes, some with decorative
relief. Free brochure.

## SMASHING TILES
425 West 13th Street
New York, NY 10014
212-633-1636
To achieve the popular *pique assiette* look,
Camille Moonsammy creates mosaics of broken tile on mesh, ready to install and grout; 40
colors, 15 patterns, in 4-, 6-, and 12-inch
squares and three border sizes. Also custom
work. Free brochure.

## SURVING STUDIOS
RD 4, Box 449
Middletown, NY 10940
800-768-4954; 914-355-1430
Natalie Surving hand-molds and hand-paints
vitrified high-relief tiles depicting naturalistic
frogs, lizards, fish, and plants; 60 designs in 7
glazes; each glaze involves 20 steps. Also custom commissions. Brochure.

## TALISMAN HANDMADE TILES
1776 West Winnemac Avenue
Chicago, IL 60640
312-784-2628
Ted Lowitz creates sculptural tile in timeless
designs such as spirals, waves, and stars.
Distributed by Ann Sacks and other retailers.
Brochure available.

## TERRA PACIFIC TILEWORKS
6566 Lincoln Street
Bloomfield, CA 94952
707-795-8827
Roger Dunham makes decorative, carved relief
tiles in several series, patterned relief borders,
corners and frames, and a broad palette of
field tile; also custom hand-painted murals.

## TILE RESTORATION CENTER
3511 Interlake North
Seattle, WA 98103
206-633-4866
Delia and Marie Glass Tapp specialize in
restoring and replicating Batchelder,
Rookwood, Grueby, Claycraft, and other vintage Arts and Crafts tile. Reproduction tiles are
sold directly and through distributors. Catalog:
$7.50.

## TOPANGA TILE STUDIO
840 Basin Drive
Topanga Canyon, CA 90290
310-455-3359
A native Australian, Leslie Doolin produces
colorful tile fish inspired by the Great Barrier
reef, including murals for swimming pools.
Represented by California Art Tile: 800-646-
8453; for custom work, contact Doolin
directly.

## PHYLLIS TRAYNOR DESIGNS, LTD.
33 Lower Trinity Pass
Pound Ridge, NY 10576
914-764-8346
Traynor molds and/or paints her own tiles or
decorates manufacturer's blanks to a client's
specifications and space.

## UDU DRUM
Route 67, Box 126
Freehold, NY 12431
518-634-2559
Frank Giorgini's handmade relief tiles have a
vigorous African look. Distributed by
Ceramica Arnon (see page 185).

## UNISON POTTERY & TILE WORKS
21103 Unison Road
Middleburg, VA 22117
540-554-8473
Joan Gardiner's majolica relief tiles are hand-
painted and depict realistic natural subjects.
Will send photographs.

## WIRTH/SALANDER STUDIOS
132 Washington Street
South Norwalk, CT 06854
203-852-9449
Georgette Wirth and Kim Salander sell colorful handmade tiles—both stock and custom-
made—from their showroom and through
distributors. Free color brochure.

# LARGE STUDIO OPERATIONS
These companies produce handcrafted tiles
in a factory setting, are able to handle large
orders, and have a wide distribution.

## EPRO, INC.
156 East Broadway
Westerville, OH 43081
614-882-6990
Largest American manufacturer of handcrafted glazed and unglazed floor and wall
tiles; numerous shapes and jewel-like colors for
inside and outdoor use; also painted decoration on high-fired terra cotta; 180 distributors.
Free 16-page catalog.

## FIREBIRD, INC.
335 Snyder Avenue
Berkeley Heights, NJ 07922
908-464-4613
Customized hand-painted flat and embossed
tiles suitable for walls and counters, depicting
animals, vegetables, flowers, fruit, butterflies,
and folk motifs; also murals. Catalog available.

## FULPER TILE, INC.
PO Box 373
Yardley, PA 19067
215-736-8512
One of the original Arts and Crafts potteries.
William Fulper III's granddaughters discov-
ered the original glaze formulas and are again
producing handmade tiles of exquisite col-
oration with crystalline or mottled effects.
Brochure: $5; 15 sample tiles: $70.

## HEATH CERAMICS, INC.
400 Gate 5 Road
Sausalito, CA 94965
415-332-3732
Fifty-year-old maker of frostproof, hand-glazed wall and floor tile in 80 opalescent colors and glossy, semigloss, matte, and semimatte surfaces; many shapes, sizes, and complete trim line; also custom glazes. Free brochure.

## MACKENZIE-CHILDS, LTD.
824 Madison Avenue
New York, NY 10021
212-570-6050
Victoria MacKenzie and Richard Childs make playful tiles to match their colorful china, glassware, and other decorative items; coordinated basins, knobs, and tile moldings. Distributed nationwide. Postcards available.

## MCINTYRE TILE COMPANY, INC.
55 West Grand Street
Healdsburg, CA 95448
707-433-8866
Glazed porcelain and stoneware floor and wall tiles in more than 200 colors. Custom services include special moldings, color development, hand painting, and murals. Literature available.

## ME TILE COMPANY
400 East Sibley Boulevard
Harvey, IL 60426
708-210-3229
Pat McGarry and Jim Evanko specialize in low-relief, hand-molded tiles in 300 styles. Many colors available, or can be glazed to match Monarch, Florida Tile, Dal-Tile, American Olean, and Summitville's white and almond field tiles. Catalog: $3.

## MORAVIAN POTTERY & TILE WORKS
Swamp Road
Doylestown, PA 18901
215-345-6722
Hand-molded, hand-painted tiles of local clay in designs created almost a century ago and inspired by astrology, nursery rhymes, Aztec and Native American cultures, medieval Europe, Bible stories, Shakespeare, and Pennsylvania Dutch stove plates. Sold by mail and at factory. Catalog available.

## PEWABIC POTTERY
10125 East Jefferson
Detroit, MI 48214
313-822-0954
One of the most renowned original Arts and Crafts companies and the supplier of many of the New York subway system tiles, Pewabic is now run as a nonprofit society and is known for its superb matte, luster, and iridescent glazes—in over 500 variations—and intricate relief work.

## SENECA TILES, INC.
7100 South County Road, 23
Attica, OH 44807
800-426-4335
Hand-molded glazed and unglazed lines, including quarry tile, in extensive array of sizes and shapes as well as trim tiles, mosaic borders, and hand-molded impressed decorative accents. Wide distribution.

## STELLAR CERAMICS
55 West Grant Street
PO Box 1321
Healdsburg, CA 95448
707-433-8166
Debbie Russell uses sand in the final firing to give tiles a rustic look. Choose from 117 glazes, most of which are transparent.

## TERRA DESIGNS, INC.
241 East Blackwell Street
Dover, NJ 07801
201-539-2999
Manufacturer of decorative wall tile and historic restoration tile and mosaics. Also has retail operation in Far Hills, NJ. Literature available.

## MAJOR MANUFACTURERS
These companies produce most of the American factory-made tile or import tile made to American designs; all are available nationwide, often through regional distribution systems that facilitate speedy delivery. Most offer literature. Call for the retailer nearest you.

## AMERICAN MARAZZI TILE, INC.
359 Clay Road
Sunnyvale, TX 75182-9710
214-226-0110
A subsidiary of the largest Italian tile manufacturer. Glazed floor and wall tile, including oversize and numerous trim pieces and stone lookalikes, are made domestically.

## AMERICAN OLEAN TILE CO.
1000 Cannon Avenue, PO Box 271
Lansdale, PA 19446-0271
215-393-2828
Large selection of glazed wall tiles and glazed and unglazed floor tile, including quarry, porcelain, and ceramic mosaics. Colors coordinate with Eljer, American Standard, and Kohler bath fixtures. Regional distribution system means most orders can be filled speedily. Video, *Design a Classic,* and two decorating pamphlets on kitchens and baths: $8. Free brochure: *How to Select & Care for Your New Ceramic Floor.*

## CROSSVILLE CERAMICS
PO Box 1168
Crossville, TN 38557
615-484-2110
Manufacturer of porcelain tile in a wide range of colors and textures; also premounted mosaic designs. Will custom-cut tile into any shape with water-jet technology. Free catalog and pamphlet, *How to Care for Porcelain Tile.*

## DAL-TILE CORPORATION
7834 Hawn Freeway
Dallas, TX 75217
800-933-TILE
Complete product lines of wall and floor tile, ceramic mosaics, porcelain, murals, stone, and pool tile. Glazed wall tile comes in a large spectrum of colors. Color coordination with major plumbing fixture companies. Free brochure and booklet, *Ceramic Tile Installation.*

## ENDICOTT TILE, LTD.
PO Box 645
Firbury, NE 68352
402-729-3323
Unglazed quarry tile and pavers. Free brochure.

**FLORIDA BRICK & CLAY CO.**
1708 Turkey Creek Road
Plant City, FL 33567
813-754-1521
Unglazed quarry tile, brick pavers, and pool
coping. Free brochure.

**FLORIDA TILE INDUSTRIES, INC.**
PO Box 447
Lakeland, FL 33802
813-687-7171
Largest American manufacturer of glazed
ceramic tile, including faux granite and marble
and handmade looks; also borders, porcelain
floor tile, and pool tile. Call for free *Color
Coordination Guide* on how to coordinate tile
with laminate, solid surfacing, and major
brands of bath fixtures. Call 800-789-TILE for
a local distributor.

**HUNTINGTON/PACIFIC
CERAMICS, INC.**
3600 Conway Street
Fort Worth, TX 76111
817-838-2323
Glazed wall tile and compatible trim. Free
literature.

**KPT, INC.**
State Road 54 East, PO Box 468
Bloomfield, IN 47424
812-384-3563
Full lines of wall and floor tile. Literature
available.

**LATCO CERAMIC TILE**
2943 Gleneden Street
Los Angeles, CA 90039
213-664-1171
Porcelain floor and wall tiles and ceramic
mosaics manufactured in Japan in 66 colors
and many shapes, including circles and triangles and trim pieces; also decorative-relief and
hand-painted tiles. Free literature.

**LAUFEN INTERNATIONAL, INC.**
Box 6600
Tulsa, OK 74156
800-758-TILE; 918-428-3851
Wide variety of wall and large-size floor tile,
including marble and terra-cotta looks; also
decorative tiles, such as reproductions of delft,
Victorian, and Art Nouveau designs.

**LONE STAR CERAMICS CO.**
PO Box 810215
Dallas, TX 75381-0215
214-247-3111
Unglazed porcelain ceramic mosaics for floors
and walls, unglazed porcelain pavers, and trim
pieces in 54 colors.

**METROPOLITAN CERAMICS**
PO Box 9240
Canton, OH 44711-9240
216-484-4887
Quarry tile and handcrafted glazed accents
that can be used indoors and out. Free catalog
and maintenance packet.

**MIDLAND INTERNATIONAL TILE**
2700 Grand Avenue
Des Moines, IA 50312
515-277-7770
Solid-color glazed wall and floor tiles in a variety of styles under brand names of Stiles and
Tileworks. Free brochure, *How to Install and
Maintain Ceramic Tile.* Send $1 and SASE for
a brochure of decorating ideas.

**MONARCH TILE, INC.**
PO Box 999
Florence, AL 35631-0999
800-BUY-TILE (289-8453); 205-764-6181
Glazed ceramic floor and wall tile, porcelain
floor tile, and ceramic mosaics; "Snaps" line is
scored to easily form triangles. Free 36-page
*Elements of Design* and installation booklets.

**QUARRY TILE COMPANY**
Spokane Industrial Park, Building 12
Spokane, WA 99216
509-924-1466
Glazed and unglazed quarry tile suitable for
interior and exterior use. Sold wherever Dal-
Tile is sold. Call for nearest distributor and free
literature.

**SUMMITVILLE TILES, INC.**
Summitville, OH 43962
216-223-1511
Quarry tile, glazed porcelain and other floor
tiles, glazed wall tiles, and pool tile. Color
coordinates to match major plumbing fixtures.
Numerous decorative tiles, including autho-
rized reproductions from Colonial
Williamsburg and tiles that coordinate with
Fitz & Floyd majolica. Custom work includes
commemorative tiles, murals, pool tile designs,
and encaustic tile.

**TERRAGREEN TECHNOLOGIES**
1650 Progress Drive
Richmond, IN 47374
317-935-4760
Glazed stoneware floor tiles for indoors and
out, which contain over 55 percent recycled
waste glass.

**UNITED STATES CERAMIC
TILE CO.**
10233 Sandyville Road, SE
PO Box 338
East Sparta, OH 44626
216-866-5531
Glazed wall tile and light-duty floor tile; exten-
sive line of accent pieces. Literature available.

**WINBURN TILE MANUFACTURING**
1790 East 9th Street, PO Box 1369
Little Rock, AR 72203-1369
501-375-7251
Unglazed porcelain ceramic mosaics. Free
brochure.

## IMPORTED TILES

Tile shops are full of both handcrafted and
factory-made imported tiles; in fact, almost
any tile made in Europe can be obtained in
this country. A few manufacturers and retailers with unique products follow. Call for
local distributors. Trade organizations provide valuable information on their country's
products.

## ARTISANOS IMPORTS, INC.
222 Gallisteo Street
Santa Fe, NM 87501
505-983-5563
Vast array of imported Mexican tile, including terra cotta, *saltillo,* and hand-painted Talavera tile with coordinated sinks, knobs, switch plate covers, etc. Mail-order catalog: $1.25

## H & R JOHNSON TILES LTD.
1912 Chattahoochee Circle
Roswell, GA 30075
770-993-6602; Fax: 770-993-0124
This large British company sells its extensive line of decorated wall and glazed floor tile through retailers nationwide. (Call 908-280-7900 for the closest distributor.) Encaustic tile in traditional multicolored patterns and solid-color coordinated "geometrics" must be ordered directly through David Malkin at the address above. Free brochure.

## ITALIAN TILE COUNCIL
Italian Trade Commission
499 Park Avenue
New York, NY 10022
Fax: 212-758-1050
Information on Italian tile and local retailers; national database provides sources for specific tiles and suggestions of appropriate tiles to use in particular applications. Free *Guide to Italian Ceramic Tile.*

## THE LIFE ENHANCING TILE COMPANY
Unit 4A, Alliance House
14-28 St. Mary's Road
Portsmouth, Hampshire
PO1 5PH United Kingdom
011-44-1705-862709
Robert Manners will sell his encaustic tiles directly. The manufacturing method used is the traditional one invented centuries ago, but designs are inspired by cultures as diverse as Peru and Persia. Write for catalog.

## PORCELANOSA USA
1301 South State College Boulevard
Anaheim, CA 92806
714-772-3183
Large Spanish manufacturer of single-fired glazed wall and floor tile widely distributed in North America. Free literature.

## SALTILLO TILE COMPANY
851 West San Mateo #8
Santa Fe, NM 87505
505-820-1830
Mexican *saltillo* floor tiles sold sealed, unsealed, stained, and whitewashed, plus 162 Talavera wall designs. Mail-order catalog: $2.

## SAM'S SOUK, INC.
979 Lexington Avenue
New York, NY 10021
212-535-7210
Sam Ben Safi imports glazed ceramic and cement "encaustic" tiles plus tile fountains from Morocco.

## TILE OF SPAIN
Trade Commission of Spain
2655 Le Jeune Road, Suite 1114
Coral Gables, FL 33134
305-446-4387
Free literature on the Spanish tile industry and retail sources.

# ANTIQUE AND OLD TILES
True antique tiles are sold by the individual piece or as a mural. Expensive, they also require special care when being installed. Other dealers specialize in tiles dating from the early twentieth century or in discontinued lines or designs. Reproduction tile makers follow sources for old and antique tiles.

## CLAIBORNE GALLERY
558 Canyon Road
Santa Fe, NM 87501
505-982-8019
Omer Claiborne sells antique Mexican tiles in his antique shop.

## GREENWICH TILE & MARBLE
38 West Putnam Avenue
Greenwich, CT 06830
203-869-1709
Michael and Vita Imbrogno operate a tile showroom and installation business. They also sell discontinued American Olean patterns and will help people locate other old tiles.

## MORTARLESS
2707 Fletcher Drive
Los Angeles, CA 90039
213-663-3291
Joe Rinniri, Jr., sells discontinued tiles by Dal-Tile; also old Franciscan, Pomona, and California Arts and Crafts firms like Batchelder, Malibu, Clay Craft, and Catalina; some antique European tiles and murals. Bring or send a sample of tile you are trying to match.

## OLD WORLD CERAMICS, INC.
1375 King Street
Greenwich, CT 06831
203-531-4608
John LeComte is a wholesaler and importer of antique decorative Dutch, Spanish, and Portuguese tiles, some as much as 400 years old, and reclaimed European terra cotta; also reproductions of traditional Dutch, Spanish, and Portuguese tiles and accessories. Antique tiles sold directly by mail; call for a local retailer of reproduction tiles. Priced literature available.

## P & E TILE
2610 San Fernando Road
Los Angeles, CA 90065
Norma Warren runs a tile contracting business but her hobby for the last 47 years has been salvaging tiles from firms that have gone out of business, including Hermosa, Pomona, Redondo, Franciscan, Interpace, and Gladding, McBean, as well as Dal-Tile discontinued designs. Clients should bring in or mail a sample of a tile they want to match; or send a clear photograph of both front and back.

## PERREAULT-RAGO GALLERY
17 South Main Street
Lambertville, NJ 08530
609-585-2546
David Rago and Suzanne Perreault sell original Grueby Faience Co. tiles in 20 different shapes and colors.

## SOLAR ANTIQUE TILE
971 First Avenue #2B
New York, NY 10022
212-755-2403
Pedro Leitao sells Portuguese and other European tiles and ceramic murals dating from the sixteenth to the early twentieth century. He also has a line of 75 reproduction Portuguese majolica tiles produced by the original fifteenth-century process. Also available at Waterworks and other retailers nationwide. Free brochure.

## HELEN WILLIAMS RARE TILES
12643 Hortense Street
Studio City, CA 91604-1107
818-761-2756
Imports seventeenth- and eighteenth-century delft, Liverpool, Spanish, and Portuguese tiles, as well as Victorian and Art Nouveau tiles. Sells individual tiles to collectors and multiples for installation. Literature upon request.

## L'ESPERANCE TILE WORKS
237 Sheridan Avenue
Albany, NY 12210
518-465-5586
See listing on page 189.

## DUTCH PRODUCTS & SUPPLY
166 Lincoln Avenue
Yardley, PA 19067
215-493-4873
Quality machine-made reproductions of crackle-glazed sixteenth- to eighteenth-century delftware in blue, magenta, and polychrome made by Westraven Pottery of the Netherlands; also hand-formed reproductions. Catalog available.

## FOURTH BAY
Box 287, 10500 Industrial Drive
Garrettsville, OH 44231
216-527-4343
Excellent reproductions of English Victorian transfer tiles.

## TILE RESTORATION CENTER
3511 Interlake North
Seattle, WA 98103
206-633-4866
See listing on page 190.

## MOSAIC ARTISTS
Although they do not typically make their own tile, artists who work with tile truly gild the lily.

## ERIN ADAMS
91 Crosby Street
New York, NY 10013
212-226-7221
Spectacular glass mosaic "rugs."

## CARLOS ALVES
1043 Lincoln Road
Miami Beach, FL 33139
305-673-3824
Alves's colorful tile murals, floors, and furniture reflect his Cuban heritage.

## BYZANTIUM MOSAIC WORKSHOP
7255 SW 48th Street
Miami, FL 33155
305-669-1670
Luciano works in both Venetian and Byzantine traditions, covering pots, walls, floors, and pools with shimmering glass mosaics. He also works in ceramic tile

## NANCY KINTISCH
3636 Brunswick
Los Angeles, CA 90039
213-666-2795; 213-663-3930
Among her many artistic endeavors, Kintisch makes magical mosaic fireplaces, fountains, rugs, and more from tile and glass.

## HOLLY LUEDERS CUSTOM MOSAICS
325 East 57th Street
New York, NY 10022
212-319-9844
Tables and custom projects using unusual whole and broken tiles. Brochure available.

## MOZAYIKS
285 Mott Street
New York, NY 10012
212-219-1160
Linda Benswanger makes *pique assiette* planters, tabletops, mirrors, and sculptures with shards of tile and porcelain. Also custom installations. Brochure available.

## PROJECTILE
4630 Saloma Avenue
Sherman Oaks, CA 91403
818-501-3614
Merle Fishman and David Catrambone use production and handmade tile to create bold, colorful mosaics on countertops, floors, fireplace surrounds, and exterior installations.

## STEPHEN SPRETNJAK
15 Laight Street
New York, NY 10013
212-431-3797
Designs and installs superb glass and ceramic mosaics.

## DEBRA YATES
7291 SW 52 Court
Miami, FL 33143
305-666-6180
Abstract painter Yates also creates large-scale mosaics from tile and other materials.

## ASSOCIATIONS
### CERAMIC TILE INSTITUTE OF AMERICA, INC.
12061 Jefferson Boulevard
Culver City, CA 90230-6219
310-574-7800
A trade organization dedicated to promoting excellence in tile installation. Works with building professionals, consults on legal issues, and offers the Ceramic Tile Consultant course. Southern California residents can call for a list of certified installers. Offers *Handbook for Ceramic Tile Installation* ($3.50, including postage) and publications on maintenance.

### NATIONAL TILE CONTRACTORS ASSOCIATION
PO Box 13629
Jackson, MS 39236
601-939-2071
A trade organization that works hand in hand with the Tile Promotion Board; will answer questions on installations and provide a list of NTCA-member installers in any locale.

## TILE COUNCIL OF AMERICA
PO Box 1787
Clemson, SC 29633-1787
803-646-TILE
An industry organization that develops installation materials and methods, monitors product standards and quality, and promotes the use of American tile to builders, architects, and homeowners. *Handbook for Ceramic Tile Installation* costs $3, plus postage.

## TILE HERITAGE FOUNDATION
PO Box 1850
Healdsburg, CA 95448
707-431-TILE
A nonprofit organization that celebrates the value of old tile, preserves worthy installations, and serves as an information network. Has a library and research facility and sells books on tile by mail. (List available upon request.) Will help find specific old tiles or modern copies. Send president Joseph Taylor a photograph and SASE. (Donations are always welcome, although not required.) Membership: $35, includes quarterly news bulletin, *Flash Point,* and biannual magazine, *Tile Heritage.*

## TILE PROMOTION BOARD
900 East Indiantown Road, Suite 211
Jupiter, FL 33477
800-495-5900; 407-743-3150
Provides consumer information and sources of domestic and imported tile. Call 800-881-8453, ext. 799, for a free 70-page source book, *The Lifestyle Is Tile,* and a list of local tile retailers who suscribe to Tile-Net.

## WORTH A VISIT
### ADAMSON HOUSE/MALIBU ART TILE MUSEUM
23200 Pacific Coast Highway
Malibu, CA 90265
310-457-8185; 310-456-8432
Built by the owners of the original Malibu Potteries and now operated as a museum, it is a monument to the beauty and versatility of tile.

## CASA DEL HERRERO FOUNDATION
1387 East Valley Road
Montecito, CA 93108
805-565-5653
Built in 1925 for George Steedman, this Spanish Colonial Revival house is now a museum, filled with a marvelous array of tile imported from Spain, Portugal, and Tunisia. By appointment only.

## THE JACKFIELD TILE MUSEUM
Ironbridge, Telford
Shropshire TF8 7AW
United Kingdom
011-44-952-882030
Situated in the original Craven Dunhill factory, the museum tells the story of the British tile industry from the 1850s to the 1960s. Tile decorating workshops available.

## MORAVIAN POTTERY & TILE WORKS
Swamp Road
Doylestown, PA 18901
215-345-6722
Henry Chapman Mercer's tile factory offers tours and a film on its history. Reservations required (call 215-348-9461) to see Fonthill, Mercer's home and now a museum of tile.

## PEWABIC POTTERY
10125 East Jefferson
Detroit, MI 48214
313-822-0954
This original Arts and Crafts supplier of many of the New York subway system tiles is once again in production and has been designated a National Historic Landmark; open Monday through Saturday.

## STRICTING FRIES AARDEWERKEMUSEUM DE WAAG
Postbus 11
8754 ZN Makkum
The Netherlands
011-31-5158-1422
Displays four centuries of tin-enameled pottery, including classic blue-and-white tiles produced in Makkum and other towns.

## TEGELMUSEUM
Eikenzoom 12
6731 BH Otterloo
The Netherlands
011-31-8382-1519
A restored farmhouse that recounts the rise of the Dutch tile industry and its subsequent decline; includes tiles dating as far back as 1300 from all over Europe.

## TILE MAINTENANCE PRODUCTS
Several companies make products for specific stain removal on tile and grout as well as sealers and cleansers. Call customer service for a local retailer.

## AQUA MIX, INC.
12940 Sunnyside Place
Santa Fe Springs, CA 90670
310-946-6877

## HILLYARD FLOOR TREATMENTS
PO Box 909
St. Joseph, MO 64502
800-365-1555

## WALTER G. LEGGE COMPANY
444 Central Avenue
Peekskill, NY 10566
800-345-3443

# Ideas to Build On

Use the grids shown on the following pages as a departure point for creating your own tile patterns. Reproduce the basic patterns that interest you on a copier machine, enlarging them if you wish, then use colored pencils or markers to design a pattern that pleases you. The smaller grids show how different coloration can give the same layout divergent personalities. Note also that the number of potential designs can be increased even further by playing with more colors or adding a border. **THIS PAGE, RIGHT:** A grid of squares is the simplest and most common pattern; contrasting colors results in a classic checkerboard design; group squares in fours for a large-scale checkerboard; alternate squares and composite squares or double up squares to make a rectangle; add another color and the possibilities multiply, as in these checkerboard variations; rotate squares 90 degrees and the "diamonds" take on a bolder personality, here in argyle and zigzag effects. **BELOW:** Framed squares, which employ slim rectangles plus small squares, or "dots," at the corners, can be formal or playful, depending on color choices; create a complex checkerboard or use a different color for each component. **OPPOSITE, TOP LEFT:** A stepped pattern employs two sizes of squares. Merely reversing colors changes the look; play with small squares in two tones or alternate colors for the larger squares. **TOP RIGHT:** The Flemish bond pattern alternates square and rectangular tiles; two colors lend a horizontal appearance, while three create a diagonal effect. **BELOW, LEFT AND RIGHT:** Either squares or rectangles can be offset in a running-bond pattern, a simpler variation of the Flemish bond.

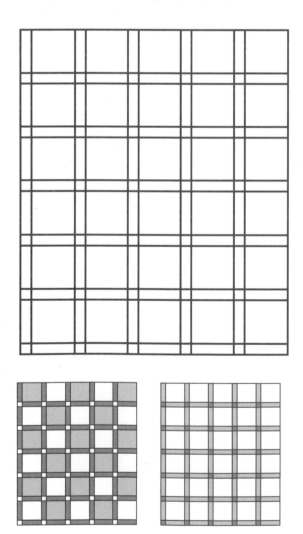

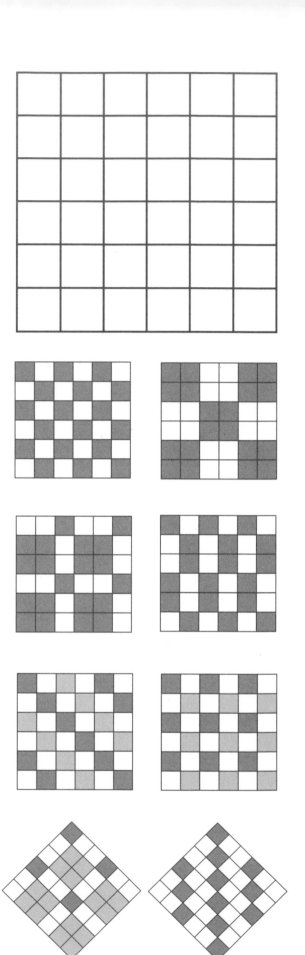

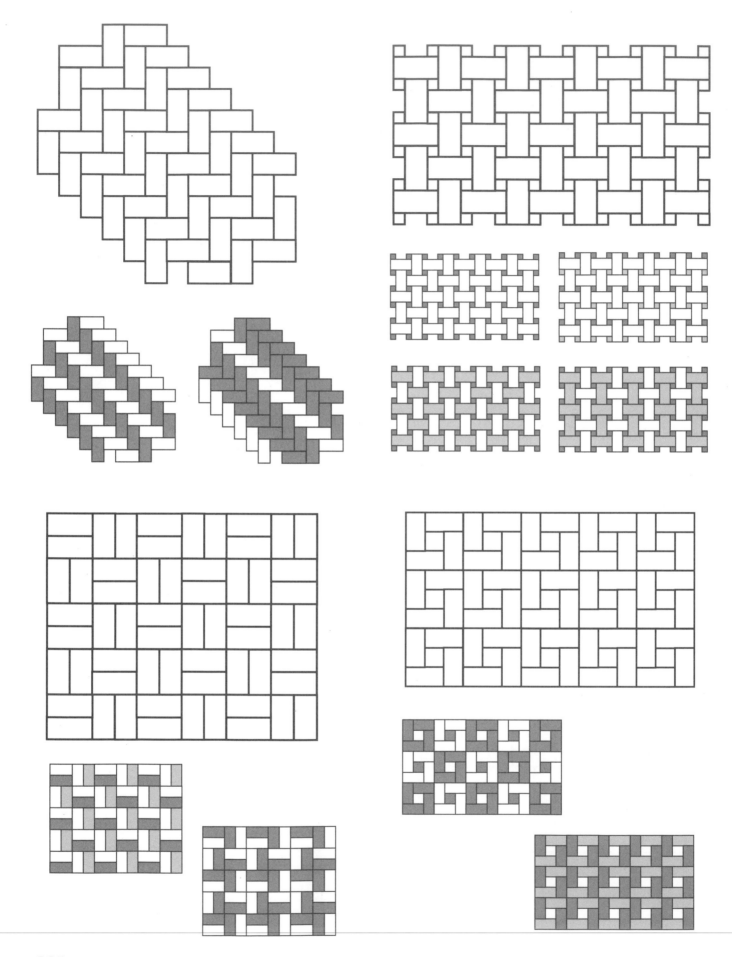

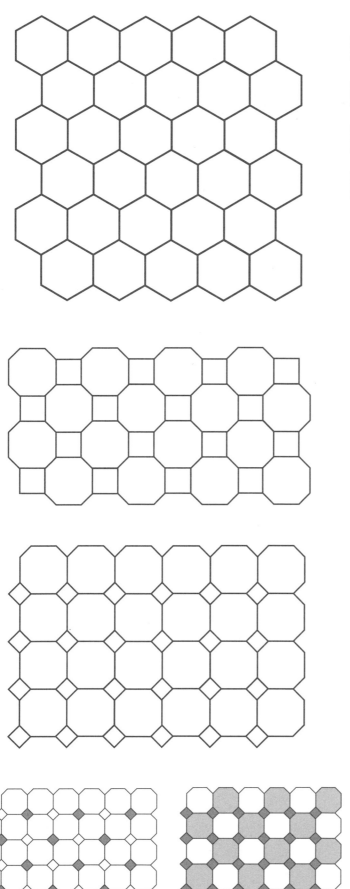

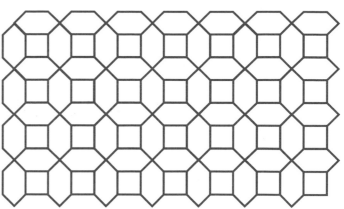

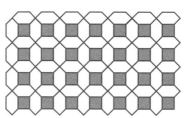

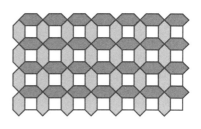

**OPPOSITE PAGE, TOP LEFT:** Place rectangles at right angles to each other to create a herringbone pattern; use one color horizontally and another vertically, or alternate single and double rows; a third variation would be to double up both colors. **TOP RIGHT:** Open lattice weave has many personalities: use one color for squares, another for rectangles, or for a subtle change, two tones for the squares; more complex patterns contrast horizontal and vertical ribbons; or alternate colors in both directions. **BOTTOM RIGHT:** A double lattice weave can be manipulated to look like either squares framing smaller squares or the warp and weft of woven fabric. **BOTTOM LEFT:** When two rectangles are laid horizontally and alternate with two laid vertically, the handsome result is called a basketweave; here, two colors create a pinwheel pattern and three suggest steps.

**THIS PAGE, LEFT, TOP TO BOTTOM:** Handsome on their own, hexagons take on different looks when two or more colors are used. Octagons paired with small squares or even smaller "dots" can be used to create classic patterns; vary the colors of the squares or dots to add interest. **ABOVE:** Elongated hexagons, or "pickets," marry with squares for a look evocative of parquet floors; in a high-contrast bicolor design, the squares seem to dominate; the tricolor example reinforces its woven and octagonal appearance.

# Acknowledgments

Hundreds of tile artisans, retailers, manufacturers, interior designers, architects, and others generously shared their knowledge, opened wide their doors, and ruffled through their Rolodexes, introducing us to more links in the tile network. Without their assistance and support, this book would not possess such range and depth.

To the undisputed president of the tile fraternity, Norman Karlson, thank you for sharing your wisdom. Ann Sacks, your ability to articulate tile's appeal was inspiring. Charlie Smallbone of Paris Ceramics provided an education on antique and hand-painted tile. Joe Taylor of the Tile Heritage Foundation served as "information central." Judith and Martin Gura, Donato Grosser and the staff of Assopiastrelli and the Italian Trade Commission, *molto grazie* for introducing us to the beauty and innovation of Italian tile. Pete Johnson of Summitville Tile and Bob Daniels of the Tile Council of America each meticulously reviewed the manuscript. Mary Levine of the Tile Promotion Board was ever helpful.

Thank you, Lori and Stephen Krause for your hospitality in Los Angeles, and to Harriette Luegge in Miami. Deep appreciation to Thurston ("Twigg"), Laila, and "Coke" Twigg-Smith, Beverly and Shaun Matthews, Bruce Jenkins, and the staff of Twin Farms. Angelique Ferrari and Lindell Lummer, thanks for introducing us to the wonderful world of Malibu tile. *Merci beaucoup* to Pierre Bergé for giving us the run of his wonderful house in St. Remy and to Charles Deméry for alerting us to tiles based on Souleiado designs. The photos were shot with the Mamiya RZ67. Thank you to Henry Froehlich, president of Mamiya American Corporation, for his technical support and encouragement.

Peter Soucy of Fired Clay Sales Strategies and Christie Stadelmaier, publisher of *Tile Distributor Newsletter*, unraveled technical details. Tile setters Arnon Zadock and David Garbo explained the intricacies of installation. Jackie Hagar of the Ceramic Tile Institute of America clarified the Ceramic Tile Consultant accreditation program. John Hoover of Bedrosian Tile explained the art and science of grout.

Special thanks to Susan Van Voorhees of American Olean, Shannon Mitchell at Florida Tile, Suzanne Edgar at Epro, Ted Lowitz of Talisman Tile, Tim Roberts of Walker Zanger, and Julie Goding of Heath Ceramics. Norma Warren of P & E Tile and Joe Rinniri of Mortarless explained how they salvage old tile and Pedro Leitao of Solar Tile gave us a firsthand glimpse at centuries-old ceramics. David Malkin of H & R Johnson and Robert Manners of the Life Enhancing Tile Company took us through the involved process of making encaustic tiles.

We are eternally in debt to the tile artists whose work makes this book a visual delight full of richness and diversity. Thank you Kathryn Allen of Kallen Architectural Ceramics; Candy Resnick and Ro Mead of Architectural Accents; Brenda Bertin; Gordon and Pam Byron of Blue Slide Art Tile; Veva Crozier; Lynda Curtis; Leslie Doolin; Anne, Rada, and Julia Fulper of Fulper Glazes; Jeff Gaines of Fire & Earth Ceramics; Frank Giorgini; Marion Grebow; Michelle Griffoul; Connie and Ronda Kay of Counterpoint Tile; Nancy Kintisch; Luciano of Byzantium Mosaic Workshop; Pat McGarry and Jim Evanko of ME Tile; Karim and Nawal Motawi; Shel Neymark; Laird Plumleigh of Alchemie Ceramic Studio; Merle Fishman and David Catrambone of Projectile; Camille Moonsammy of Smashing Tiles; Stephen Spretnjak; Ron Stritz and Genevive Sylvia of Pewabic Pottery; Phyllis Traynor; Tom and Diana Watson of Native Tile & Ceramics; Dale Wiley of À Mano; and Adam Zayas of Moravian Pottery & Tile Works.

On the retail front, thank you to Sunny McLean; Janet Feher, Marcie Feigen, Sheri Hirschfeld, and Scott Chavkin of Ann Sacks Tile & Stone; Douglas Karlson, Suzanne Spahn, and Joost de Quack of Country Floors; Barbara and Peter Sallick of Waterworks; Juri Marinkovich of The Studio; and Nola Stucky of NS Ceramics. Thank you also to Cheryl Blakely of Busby Gilbert/Malibu Tile Group; Ken Rossomando of Elon; Mark Shedrofsky of Design Supply; Michael Weber of Tiles: A Refined Selection; Richard Goddard and Karen Bishop of Concept Studio; Shep Brown; and Brian Flynn and Susi Parker.

To the designers and architects who melded their aesthetic vision with the beauty of fired clay, we appreciate your help. Thank you, Christine Andigier; Laurinda Spear, Bernardo Fort-Brescia, and Richard Talbert of Arquitectonica; Nathalie Badakian; Linda Banks; Douglas R. Bartoli; Sophie and Hugues Bosc; Eleanor Brenner; Dana Cantelmo; Phillipe Eckert; Beverly Ellsley; Harry Elson and Jason Gold; Stephen and Gail Huberman; Gail Green; Anne James; Dennis Jenkins; Jed Johnson, Vance Burke, and John Clauson of Jed Johnson & Associates; Raymond Jungles; Terry Levan Katz; Holly Leuders; Deborah Lipner; Llana of Lemeau & Llana; Kevin Mayo and Ralph DeLucci; Richard Mervis; Marin Scott Milam and Hank Milam; Nall; Florence Perchuk; Joan Picone of European Country Kitchens; Van-Martin Rowe; Fernando Sanchez and Maria Eugenia Mendez-Penate of The Pineapple Designs; Alan Wanzenberg and Scott Cornelius of Alan Wanzenberg Architects; and Debra Yates.

Without the homeowners who welcomed us into their houses—and their lives—*Tiles* simply would not exist. We are eternally grateful to the following homeowners: Leslie and Rutgers Barclay, Carolina Barrie, Ernest Biscardi, Carol and Andrew Boas, Kelly and

Dan Bourgoise, Laurinda and Pat Cauley, Bob Cowart, Chris and James Cowperthwaite, Mary and Peter Dooney, Zoe and John Eisenberg, Mitzie and Warren Eisenberg, Linda Engel, Sue and Leonard Feinstein, Marilyn and Ray Frankel, Martiza and Pedro Garcia-Carrillo, Sandy and Michael Garrett, Fred Goldstein, Julie and Stan Harfenist, Judite and Adam Haut, Jean and Doug Hill, Sandra and Max Hulse, Erica Jesselson, Douglas Johnson, Maureen and Bruce Johnston, Dee Juergens and Betty Meyers, Bobbie Katzander, Stella and Len Kleinrock, Esther Korman, Jonathan Lewis, Andrea and Jeffrey Lomasky, Karen Loud, Sharon and Hobbes Marlowe, Tom Masi and Susan Pignotti, Jacqui Matthews, Karen McCammon and Christopher McGratty, Dawn and Steve Miller, Phyllis Miriam, James Orr, Phoebe and Adams Perry, Lynn Richardson and Armin Müller, Jane and Jack Rivkin, Gloria and Harry Sanchez, Adrienne and James Schettino, Edie and Ernie Schwartz, Jimmy Seitz, Tori Warner and David Shepherd, Joan and Dan Speirs, Estelle and Fred Stein, Morton Swinsky, Peter Ticchelaerr, Liza and Edward Weihman, Carole and Hugh Westbrook, Barbara Windom, and Bonnie and Gary Ziegler.

Russ Guiney and Lynette Hernandez of the California Department of Parks & Recreation and docent Rosemary Hoppe made it possible for us to photograph the spectacular Adamson House in Malibu. Laura Bridley welcomed us to the Casa del Herrero in Montecito. In the Netherlands, the curators of the Otterloo Tile Museum and of the Fries Aardewerkemuseum in Makkum were equally gracious in allowing us access.

Thank you, Susan Becher, Rose Gilbert, and Mike Strohl, for your friendship and support from the start. Andy Warren, Steve Piersol, Edward Claiborne, Greg Voight, and Greg Richards were brilliant in their lighting assistance, to say nothing of working long hours and schlepping all the photography equipment.

When this book was just a proposal, we took it to one and only one publisher, knowing that Clarkson Potter was the best house for a heavily photographic book on a design-oriented subject. Thank you, Lauren Shakely, for having the vision to see that this book could be beautiful *and* fact-filled. We were blessed with editor Pam Krauss, who is both card-carrying member of the tile lovers' society and a meticulous unraveler of a manuscript that kept wanting to go in a circle rather than a straight line; she understood when to push and when to pull back, and was always sensitive to working with coauthors separated by two thousand miles. Art director Howard Klein and designer Renato Stanisic shared our vision for a book that was lush and playful. Thank you for intuitively understanding that an elegantly simple design would let the photos tell the story. Margot Schupf cheerfully helped in myriad small ways. Mark McCauslin and Joan Denman shepherded the book through production.

If there is a saint of patience and forbearance, surely she must be our wonderful agent, Helen Pratt. Throughout the two-year process of preparing this book, she endured late-night and early-morning calls from not one but two authors. Thank you, Helen, for your wisdom, calm, and humor. You always kept us focused on the most important task—how to make this book the best it could be.

On the home front, thank you to our husbands for putting up with spouses who were frequently on the road—and when they weren't, often spent their weekends working. It must have seemed at times as if we were married to each other rather than to each of you! You gave us the gift of freedom, plus sage advice and hot meals. Ron Buehl's careful reading of the manuscript at its earliest stages helped immeasurably. Landt Dennis's dialing for designers made all the difference in Santa Barbara.

Finally, we acknowledge each other for planting the seed of an idea in the fertile soil of professional respect and allowing an enduring partnership and true friendship to blossom.

# Credits

Designers and architects' addresses are given after their first mention. Addresses for tile manufacturers, artisans, retailers, and mosaic artists are listed under the appropriate headings in the Directory of Resources. We have made every effort to identify tiles shown in photographs, relying on information provided by designers or homeowners. In the case of antique and old installations, information is usually not available. Check under Antique and Old Tiles in the Directory of Resources on page 193 to find companies that may carry similar old or reproduction tiles. Vendors for many projects are listed; contact the manufacturer or artisan for vendors in your region.

Jacket: Malibu Potteries fountain at the Adamson House/Malibu Tile Museum.

Cover: 4- and 2-inch-square Shadow Square tiles by Talisman Handmade Tile, from Ann Sacks Tile & Stone.

Endpapers: Design by Douglas R. Bartoli of Bartoli Design, 825 Santa Barbara St., Santa Barbara, CA 93101; 805-963-6125. Tile by Moore-Merkowitz, from NS Ceramic.

Page 1: Mosaic leaf tiles by Michelle Griffoul, from Ann Sacks Tile & Stone.

2: Design by Bill Willis, Marrakesh, Morocco; phone: 011-212-4-442-457.

3: Mosaic design by Shel Neymark.

4: Andalucia Ronda border, 4-inch by 8-inch Metro, Marbella border, and 5½-inch by 11-inch tile, from Ann Sacks Tile & Stone.

5 *left:* Design by Sophie and Hugues Bosc, 38 Boulevard Victor Hugo, 13210 Saint Remy de Provence, France; 011-33-90-92-10-81. Tile fragments on dog house; Moroccan cement tile imported by Carocim, Quartier Beaufort CD 14, 13540 Puyricard, France; phone: 011-33-42-92-20-39. *Right:* 4-inch Mexican brush-glazed tiles from Counterpoint Tile.

6: Mola relief tile by Dale Wiley of À Mano.

10: Design by Nathalie Badakian. Tiles by Masterceram, Zac du Roubian, 13150 Tarascon, France; Fax: 011-33-90-91-31-93.

11: Victorian transferware tiles, from The American Country Collection, 620 Cerrillos Road, Santa Fe, NM 87501; 505-984-0955.

**Fundamental Matters**

14: Design by Teri Levan Katz of Vanguard Interiors, 11055 Girasol Avenue, Coral Gables, FL 33156; 305-661-4451. Hand-painted Dat-Faenza tiles and trims, from Sunny McLean & Co.

15 *left:* Design by Jean and Douglas Hill, French Country Living, Rue des Remparts, 06250 Mougins, France. *Right:* Italian majolica Florentino border by Walker Zanger.

16: Calao 6-inch-square glazed relief tile with footprint borders, by L. Curtis Designs.

17 *left:* Design by Kevin B. De Mayo and Ralph DeLucci of Mayo DeLucci Interiors, 405 East 54th Street, Suite 9E, New York, NY 10022; 212-752-2762. White pavers accented with ceramic mosaics, from Hastings Tile & Il Bagno. *Right:* Interior design by Jed Johnson and project designer Vance Burke, of Jed Johnson & Associates, Inc. Architecture: Alan Wanzenberg and project architect Scott Cornelius, of Alan Wanzenberg Architects, P.C., both at 211 West 61st Street, New York, NY 10023; 212-489-7840. Tile by Moravian Pottery & Tile Works. Photographed at Twin Farms in Barnard, Vermont.

18 *top row, left and center: Bestiare et Genie* series and *Animaux et Divinites* series tiles, both by L. Curtis Designs. *Top row, right:* Malibu Revival tile from Walker Zanger. *Second row, left:* 8-inch-square relief cowboy tile by Alchemie Ceramic Studio. *Second row, right:* Triclino mural by L. Curtis Designs. *Third row, left:* Malibu Revival tile; and *third row, center:* Batchelder Peacock panel from the Stonecreek collection, both from Walker Zanger. *Third row, right:* Encaustic tiles from The Life Enhancing Tile Company. *Bottom row, left:* LV Miradouro hand-painted fruit basket panel from Portugal, from Country Floors. *Bottom row, center:* Hand-molded tile by Dale Wiley of À Mano. *Bottom row, right:* Art Nouveau 6-inch square AM Poppy tile by Busby Gilbert, from Ann Sacks Tile & Stone.

19: 8-inch square glazed dragonfly relief tile by Motawi Tileworks.

20 *left:* 2-inch-square glazed tiles by Pewabic Pottery. *Right:* Design by Harry Elson and Jason Gold of Elson & Gold Architects, 250 West 57th Street, New York, NY 10107; 212-265-3535. Luster glazed tiles by Fire & Earth, from Ann Sacks Tile & Stone.

21: 4-inch-square glazed tiles by Surving Studios, from From the Ground Up.

22-23: 4-inch-square Mexican Talavera Midnight Blue solid color and design #87, from Artisanos.

25: Interior design by Jed Johnson and project designer Vance Burke, of Jed Johnson & Associates, Inc. Architecture: Alan Wanzenberg and project architect Scott Cornelius, of Alan Wanzenberg Architects, P.C. All tile custom designed by the architects and produced by Peace Valley Tiles. Photographed at Twin Farms in Barnard, Vermont.

26 *left:* Tile design by Joost de Quack of Country Floors. All tiles handmade by WT Coloratura, from Country Floors. *Right:* Design by Linda Banks of Banks Design Associates, Ltd. 176 West Norwalk Road, Norwalk, CT. 06850; 203-854-5060, and Caren McCammon McGratty of CMC II Interiors, 4424 Potomac Drive, Dallas, TX 75205; 214-526-8240. 6-inch-square Intaglio tile in pewter-finish, from Ann Sacks Tile & Stone.

27: Hand-molded stoneware Afro Series tiles by Frank Giorgini of Udu Drum, from Ceramica Arnon.

28: Hand-molded and hand-painted 8-inch by 10-inch tiles by Marion Grebow; calligraphy by Moki Kokoris.

29: Design by Kitchens by Deane, 1267 East Main Street, Stamford, CT 06902; 203-327-7008. Handpainted tiles by Phyllis Traynor of Designs, Ltd.

30 *top:* Mosaic tiles by Michelle Griffoul, from Ann Sacks Tile & Stone. *Bottom:* Arts & Crafts Glaze collection, from Ann Sacks Tile & Stone.

**Putting It All Together**

32: Design by Fernando Sanchez of The Pineapple Designs, Inc., 326 Menores, Coral

Gables, FL 33134; 305-445-9591. Reproduction William De Morgan tiles, from Country Floors.

33 *left:* Celtic Old English medallion hand-molded by Motawi Tileworks. *Right:* Seville Madagas border in bronze metallic luster glaze by Walker Zanger.

36-37: See page 25 credit.

38-39: Design by Douglas Johnston, 8 Rue des Cordelliers, Fortcalquier, Provence, France 04300.

40: Tile design by Joost de Quack, CTC, Country Floors. WT Coloratura handmade wall tiles in niche; PN Provençal rustic glazed and unglazed terra-cotta floor tiles, imported from France, and Tile Guild's hand-painted Maroc tile on near wall, all from Country Floors.

41: Design by Eleanor Brenner of Brenner & Allen, 505-989-9081. 4-inch-square pillowed tile imported from Italy by Nova Tile.

42 *top:* Design by Gail Green, Ltd. 110 East 59th Street, New York, NY 10022; 212-909-0376. 8-inch-square "Key Point" tiles (fitted with stainless steel grommets) by Bardelli, sink, and fittings, all imported from Italy by Hastings Tile & Il Bagno. *Center:* Design by Terri Levan Katz of Vanguard Interiors. Handmade glazed terra-cotta tile by Demuth Napa Valley Tile, from Sunny McLean & Co. *Bottom:* Hand-molded oak leaf and acorn border, 2-inch cornice, and 4-inch-square field tile by The Meredith Collection.

43: Vanilla glazed Lunarstone Series ceramic mosaics by Dal-Tile.

44-45: Design by Gail Green Ltd. 8-inch-square Bardelli Bianco glossy white wall tiles; accented with 4-inch-square Window tiles by Artgiana, both imported from Italy; and filled with 2-inch-square Lyric Stone tiles made of polished violet oyster and nautilus shells, imported from the Philippines; 8-inch-square Italian white matte floor tile, black border, fixtures and fittings, all from Hastings Tile & Il Bagno.

46: Design by John Watson Architect, 726 Chelham Way, Montecito, CA, 93108; 805-969-7280. Tile design: Juri Marinkovich of The Studio. MS Seville 5½-inch by 11-inch tile, from The Studio.

47: Interior design by Van-Martin Rowe Design Studio. Walls and floors of Appiani white ceramic tiles and Northwest Glass tiles and mosaics, all from Ann Sacks Tile & Stone.

48: Design by Diane Provenzano of Doris LaPorte Design, 40 West 77th Street, New York, NY 10024; 212-874-6751. Tile and ceramic mosaic from American Olean. Custom plasterwork by Stephen Balser of Art in Construction, 8 Beach Street, New York, NY 10013; 212-334-5227.

49: Stained, sealed, and whitewashed Mexican terra cotta, from Artisanos.

51: Design by A. J. Loeffler, Loeffler Johansen Bennett Architects, 821 Broadway, New York, NY 10003; 212-475-6800. Relief border, tile, molding, and ceramic mosaics by Blue Slide Art Tile Co., from Waterworks.

52-53: Design by Joan Picone of European Country Kitchens, 49A Route 202/Minebrook Road, Far Hills, NJ 07931; 908-781-1554. Backsplash of relief tiles by Moore-Merkowitz, from Ann Sacks Tile & Stone.

54: Design by Dana Cantelmo Architect, 1710 Monterey Blvd., Hermosa Beach, CA 90254; 310-318-8883. Tile design: Janet McHugh, CTC, Country Floors. Hand-molded tile by WC California Series, from Country Floors.

55 *top:* Orielle cornice, rope, and diamond liner in Peridot; dots in Peacock and Amazon; terra-cotta dolphins tile antiqued with aquamarine grout, all from Walker Zanger. *Second from top:* Hand-painted tile by Veva Crozier of Lukkens Color. *Second from bottom:* 4-inch hexagons in assorted colors by Epro, from Ann Sacks Tile & Stone. *Bottom:* Handcrafted "Metallo" series tile in Bronze by Walker Zanger.

**On the Floor**

56 Mexican *saltillo* floor tile from Saltillo Tile Company. Glazed tile on fireplace from Counterpoint Tile.

57 *left:* Heritage and Intricates tiles by Epro. *Right:* Monaldeschi deco border in Tagina Umbria Series by Walker Zanger.

58: See page 55 second from bottom credit.

59: See page 25 credit.

60 *top right:* Handmade terra-cotta *provençals* by London Ceramics, available at Ann Sacks Tile & Stone. *Center left:* Antique French terra cotta and border of new Torquemada terra cotta, both from Ann Sacks Tile & Stone. *Center right:* Design by Nathalie Badakian. Glazed pale gray, floral border, and terra cotta tiles, all by Masterceram. *Bottom left:* Design by Sophie and Hugues Bosc. French terra cotta and glazed terra cotta by Carocim. *Bottom right:* Design by Nathalie Badakian. Terra-cotta tiles by Masterceram.

61: Harvard Square Ironrock flashed quarry tiles with Heather Blue glazed Metro accents, both by Metropolitan Ceramics.

62: Design by Michele Michael, 184 Concord St., Brooklyn, NY 11201; 718-855-0152. Travertino and Brenta Green squares accented with Ebony stars cut by water jet, all in porcelain tile from the Verandah Collection by Crossville Ceramics.

63: See page 25 credit.

64: Glazed hand-painted tiles from Paris Ceramics.

65 *left:* Italian encaustic tiles from Country Floors. *Right:* Cement tiles made in Morocco and imported to France by Carocim.

68: Design by Van-Martin Rowe Design Studio. Multicolor tiles by Appiani and hand-painted Dana's Sketchbook central tile, both from Ann Sacks Tile & Stone.

69 *top:* Tile design by Joost de Quack, CTC, Country Floors. Hand-molded WS solid-color field tile and Tile Guild's hand-painted Maroc tiles, both from Country Floors. *Bottom:* Terra-cotta elongated hexagons, limestone squares, and glazed ceramic insert, all from Ann Sacks Tile & Stone.

70-71: Mosaic design by Nancy Kintisch.

72: Design by Sam Robin of Sam Robin Interior Design, 1000 Venetian Way, Suite 112, Miami, FL. 33139, 305-375-0727. Tile design: Luciano for Byzantium Mosaic Workshop. Cement tile imported from the Yucatan by Sunny McLean & Co.

74: Glazed, unglazed, and whitewashed terra-cotta tile, from Country Floors. Similar rug fringe tiles available from Walker Zanger.

75: Two-part fish-shaped ceramic tiles and mosaics by Michelle Griffoul; and leaf-green slate, both from Ann Sacks Tile & Stone.

76: Design by Jean-Michel Quincey of JMQ Design, 460 West 24th Street, Suite 5A, New York, NY 10011; 212-645-7479. Mosaic design: Stephen Spretnjak. Venetian glass Vetricolor ¾-inch mosaics by Bisazza Mosaico from Nemo Tile and glass droplets from Bendheim Glass, 122 Hudson Street, New York, NY 10002; 212-226-6370.

77: Design and handmade tile by Ro Mead and Candy Resnick of Architectural Accents.

**In the Kitchen**

78: Design by Holly Leuders, 325 East 57th Street, New York, NY 10022; 212-319-9844. Reproduction English Victorian tiles by L'Esperance Tileworks.

79 *left:* Kitchen design by Beverly Ellsley,

of Beverly Ellsley Collection, 175 Post Road, Westport, CT 06880; 203-454-0503. Interior design by Randi Filoon, of Katherine Cowdin, Inc., 3 East Elm Street, Greenwich, CT 06830; 203-661-4844. Crackle glazed and hand-painted tiles from Paris Ceramics. *Right:* Hand-painted Spanish *culinarios,* from Country Floors.

80: Custom hand-painted topiary tile by Christine Belfour Design, Ltd., 177 East 87th Street, Studio 402, New York, NY 10128; 212-722-5410.

81: Sailboat 4-inch-square glazed tiles from Native Tile & Ceramics.

82-83: Design by A. J. Loeffler, Loeffler Johansen Bennett Architects. Hand-molded and handpainted tile and ceramic mosaics by Blue Slide Art Tile, from Waterworks.

84 *left:* Design by Van-Martin Rowe Design Studio. White counter tile, 2-inch half-round molding, and multicolor backsplash tile, all by Appiani, from Ann Sacks Tile & Stone. *Right:* Crystalline glazed tile and bullnose trim from Ann Sacks Tile & Stone.

85 *left:* Wine label decal tiles and field tile. Similar product available from Tiles: A Refined Selection. *Right:* Design by Eleanor Brenner of Brenner & Allen. 4-inch Italian tile and V-cap edge trim, from Nova Tile.

86-87: Kitchen design by Beverly Ellsley, Handcrafted cabinets from The Beverly Ellsley Collection.

88-89: Solid color tiles and mosaic ceramics by Brenda Bertin. Portuguese Sasha scenic wall tiles from Country Floors.

90: Design by Harry Elson and Jason Gold of Elson & Gold Architects. Luster-glazed blue (niche) and green (backsplash) tiles by Fire & Earth, from Ann Sacks Tile & Stone. Cabinets by McGrame Woodworking.

91: See page 20 left credit.

92 *top left:* Michelle Griffoul mosaics, from Ann Sacks Tile & Stone. *Top right:* See page 79 left credit. Kitchen cabinets by The Beverly Ellsley Collection. *Center left:* Design by Kitchens by Deane. Adirondack tile from Country Floors. *Center right:* Design by Gail and Stephen Huberman of SGH Designs, 21 Pond Pass, Woodbury, NY 11797; 516-364-1770. Field tile from Hastings Tile & Il Bagno; hand-painted topiary tile by Christine Belfour Design, Ltd. *Bottom left:* See page 26 right credit. *Bottom right:* Design by Christian Andigier, Mas Violet, Chemin Jean Piquet, 13210 St. Remy de Provence, France. Mexican

Talavera tiles from Globe Trotter; similar product available from Elon Tile.

93 *top left:* Mosaic tile mural by Candy Resnick and Ro Mead of Architectural Accents. *Top right:* Design by Holly Leuders. Mold-pressed tiles from Moravian Pottery and Tile Works. *Center:* Hand-painted chicken mural by Veva Crozier of Lukkens Color. *Bottom left:* See page 14 credit. *Bottom right:* Design by Dorothy McCord Smith, 1114 Hickox Street, Santa Fe, NM 87501; 505-982-9781. Boa Vista Portuguese hand-painted Les Flores Glandes wall tile, from Country Floors.

94-95: Design by Fernando Sanchez of The Pineapple Design. Boa Vista white and hand-painted Portuguese wall tiles in blue and white Obidos design with matching border tiles; *culinarios* vegetable panels behind range; Miradouro Portuguese Cirro sponge-design tile on counters, and all trims, from Country Floors. Accessories from Antiques and Collectibles by Us, 4703 S.W. 72nd Avenue, Miami, FL 33155; 305-361-0042.

96-97: Design by Joan Picone of European Country Kitchens. Hand-painted Spanish *culinarios* and cobalt blue tiles, both from Country Floors. Cabinets by Peer & Picone Woodworks.

97 *right:* Design by Kitchens by Deane. Handpainted tile on backsplash and range hood by Phyllis Traynor of Designs, Inc.; Talavera tile on counter from Elon.

98: Design by Joan Picone of European Country Kitchens. Scrolling vine relief tile on range hood by Talisman Handmade Tiles; backsplash of tumbled marble squares inset with glazed relief tiles by Moore-Merkowitz, both from Ann Sacks Tile & Stone. Cabinets by Peer & Picone Woodworks.

99: Design by Hank Milam and Miran Scott Milam of Hank Milam & Associates, 24325 Cimmaron Court, Laguna Niguel, CA, 92677; 714-831-6513. Hand-painted Miradouro Portuguese tile depicting camelias and vases, cherub panels behind range, and decorative trims and molding, all from Country Floors.

100-101: Design by Anne James, 611 Orchard Avenue, Santa Barbara, CA 93108; 805-969-4554. Mexican Talavera tile from Ann Sacks Tile & Stone. Cabinets crafted by Mark C. Steward, 250 B. Industrial Way, Buellton, CA 93427.

**In the Bath**

102: Design by Sophie and Hugues Bosc.

Similar Provençal tiles available at Ann Sacks Tile & Stone.

103 *left:* Relief tiles by Blue Slide Art Tile, from Waterworks. *Right:* Orielle leaf border in Peridot and Fresca terra-cotta liner antiqued with aquamarine grout, both from Walker Zanger.

104-105: Design by Michael Morrison Designs, 417 North San Vicente Blvd., Los Angeles, CA 90048; 310-657-8748. Tile design: Doreen Reale of From the Ground Up. AB glazed tile in custom color Honey, AB liners and ceramic mosaics in Purple, and liners in Gloss TC #81, with tumbled marble tiles, all from From the Ground Up.

106: Design by Sam Robins of Sam Robins Interior Design. Mosaic design: Luciano for Byzantium Mosaic Workshop. Venetian glass mosaics by Mosaicos Venecianos de Mexico from Byzantium Mosaic Workshop.

107: Hand-molded and hand-painted tile by Ronda and Connie Kay of Counterpoint Tile.

108-109: Design by Dana Cantelmo Architect. Tile design: Janet McHugh, CTC, Country Floors. Hand-molded tile, all trim, and ceramic accessories in Malibu Sand, Calais, Persimmon, and Christmas Red by WC California Series from Country Floors.

110-111: English reproduction William De Morgan and William Morris tiles, bathtub, and fittings, all from Waterworks.

112: Interior design by Lynn Richardson. Tile design: Nola Stucky of NS Tile. Field tile, borders, and trim, reproduced from Malibu Potteries designs by Native Tile & Ceramics.

113 *left:* Design by Van-Martin Rowe Design Studio. Cream-color 8-inch-square handmade Mexican tiles, and multicolor tiles by Ken Mason, both from Country Floors. *Top right:* Design by Richard Mervis Design, Inc., 654 Madison Avenue, New York, NY 10021; 212-371-6396. Tile design: Joost de Quack, CTC, Country Floors. WC hand-molded wall tiles in green, white, and silver, metallic moldings, and tumbled marble tiles on floor, all from Country Floors. *Lower right:* Deborah T. Lipner of Deborah T. Lipner, Ltd., One Fawcett Place, Greenwich, CT 06830; 203-629-2212. All tile by Walker Zanger, from Waterworks.

114: See page 25 credit.

115 *top:* See page 46 credit. *Center:* See page 113 left credit. *Bottom:* Luster-glazed tile and trim, from Counterpoint Tiles.

116-117: Architecture by Jean-Michel Quincey of JMQ Design. Mosaic design: Stephen Spretnjak. Venetian glass Vetricolor ¾-inch mosaics by Bisazza Mosaico from Nemo Tile.

118 *left:* Reproductions of Julia Morgan's Deer Creek relief tiles, from Waterworks. *Right:* See page 25 credit.

119: Green Blue Silver Gold luster tile by Fire & Earth, from Ann Sacks Tile & Stone.

120: Design by A. J. Loeffler, Loeffler Johansen Bennett Architects. Wall and floor tile, ceramic mosaics, and Critter borders, by Blue Slide Art Tile, from Waterworks.

121: Design by Deborah T. Lipner of Deborah T. Lipner, Ltd. Wall tiles and Elephant Walk border all by Blue Slide Art Tile, from Waterworks; floor tile by American Olean.

122: Design by Gail Green of Gail Green Ltd. Tumbled marble mosaic designed by Gail Green, white Italian tile, sink, and fittings, all from Hastings Tile & Il Bagno.

123 *top:* Design by Deborah T. Lipner of Deborah T. Lipner, Ltd. Terra-cotta border by Walker Zanger from Waterworks. *Bottom:* See pages 44–45 credit.

124: Design by Linda White of White Designs, 9 Wave Crest, Venice, CA 90291; 310-581-5588. Leaf mosaics by Michelle Griffoul.

125: Interior design by Ronni Fallows of Ronni Fallows Design, 827 Camino del Poniente, Santa Fe, NM 87501; 505-989-3895. Hand-molded tile mural by Shel Neymark.

126-127: Design by Dennis Jenkins, 5813 SW 68th Street, Miami, FL 33143; 305-665-6960. Mexican *saltillos,* Cantera stone, and similar French glazed ogees, from Sunny McLean & Co.

**Around the House**

128: Design by Sophie and Hugues Bosc. Moroccan cement tiles imported to France by Carocim.

129 *left:* See page 25 credit. *Right:* Ravena liner and Orielle Amazon rounded liner from the Musa Series by Walker Zanger.

130: Antique painted Mexican terra-cotta tile from Claiborne Gallery.

131: Design by Hank Milam and Miran Scott Milam of Hank Milam & Associates. Mexican Talavera tile from Artisanos.

132: Design by Dennis Jenkins. Universe and field tiles with star corners by DAT Faenza, from Sunny McLean & Co.

133: Design by Beverly Ellsley. All tile from Country Floors.

134–135: Antique Royal Makkum tiles. Reproductions sold at Country Floors.

136-137 Design by Holly Leuders. Encaustic and glazed tiles from L'Esperance Tile Works.

139 *top left:* See endpapers credit. *Top right:* Design by Holly Leuders. Tiles from L'Esperance Tile Works. *Bottom left:* Tiles hand-painted by Veva Crozier of Lukkens Color. *Bottom right:* Design by Holly Leuders. Tile by Pratt & Larsen.

140-141: Design by Holly Leuders. Glazed tiles on stair risers by L'Esperance, Pratt & Larsen, and Moravian Pottery and Tile Works. Florentine mosaic tile on chimney breast, field tile on fireplace surround, and tile letters also by Moravian Pottery and Tile Works.

143 *top right:* Design by Dorothy McCord Smith. Antique Delft tile murals. *Bottom right:* Antique Mexican tiles from The Claiborne Gallery.

144: Mexican brush-glazed tile from Counterpoint Tile.

145 *top:* Shaped tiles copied from fabric design by Ronda and Connie Kay of Counterpoint Tiles. *Center:* Design and hand-painted tiles by Nall, The Nall Institute, Vence, Provence, France. *Bottom:* See page 106 credit.

146: Mexican field tile from Artisanos; border and inset of spiral and wave relief tile by Talisman Handmade Tiles.

147: Tile mural hand-painted by Marion Grebow on 6-inch-square bisque blanks.

**The Great Outdoors**

148: Design by Hugues and Sophie Bosc. Antique terra cotta with glazed squares by Carocim on floor. *Zellij* table from Morocco.

149 *left:* Architecture by Laurinda Spear and Bernardo Fort-Brescia, of Arquitectonica, 426 Jefferson Avenue, Miami Beach, FL 33139; 305-672-0096. Hand-painted tiles by Mary Grabill; field tiles by American Olean. *Right:* Santa Cruz border from Capistrano series by Walker Zanger.

150 *top:* Pietra, Saxum, Later, and Tellus foot-square tiles by Monoceram, from Ann Sacks Tile & Stone. *Bottom:* Design by Van-Martin Rowe Design Studio. Appiani tile in assorted colors, from Ann Sacks Tile & Stone.

151: Architecture by Laurinda Spear and Bernardo Fort-Brescia, of Arquitectonica. Tile by American Olean.

154 *top:* See page 106 credit. *Bottom left:* Stair design by Angelique Ferrari of Malibu Art Tile. Hand-molded decorative tiles by Malibu Art Tile; terra-cotta tiles by Western Quarry Tile, 490 East Duarte Rd., Monrovia, CA 91016; 818-358-2465.

155: Design by Van-Martin Rowe Design Studio. Multicolor tiles by Ken Mason, from Country Floors.

156-157: Design by Dennis Jenkins. Brazilian and broken tile on columns, address plaque, Spanish checkerboard tiles, Spanish tarot card tiles, and Turkish tile depicting horseman, all from Sunny McLean & Co.

158: Cement tiles imported from Morocco to France by Carocim.

159 *top:* Design by Dennis Jenkins. Brazilian and broken tile on cement bench, from Sunny McLean & Co. *Center:* Design by Lynn Richardson.

160-161: Landscape architecture and pool design by Raymond Jungles, ASLA, 7291 SW 52nd Court, South Miami, FL 33143; 305-666-9299. Mosaic design: Debra Yates.

161: Design by Dennis Jenkins. Antique English tiles from Country Floors.

162: Mosaic design: Merle Fishman and David Catrambone of Projectile Studio. Mosaic made of broken Busby Gilbert tiles; pool tiles by American Universal Tile.

163: See page 106 credit.

166: Design by Fernando Sanchez, The Pineapple Designs, Inc. Mosaic installation: Vernays Rodriguez. Green and white marble and terra cotta, all from Country Floors.

167: Design by Nathalie Badakian. Terra-cotta tiles by Masterceram.

168: Mosaic design by Shel Neymark.

170-185: All tiles by Walker Zanger.

# Index